HILARY A.

THE SECOND PIECE OF FRENCH TOAST

Dear Ginger & Adam,

Thank you for contributing your gift of healing and helping me to create a happy, healthy & fabulous life.

I love you —
Hilary

© Hilary Arnow Burns, 2019
ISBN 978-0-578-61614-8

All rights reserved. No part of this publication may be reproduced or transmitted in any form or by any means, electronic or mechanical, including photocopying, recording, or any information storage retrieval system, without prior permission in writing from the publisher.

No responsibility for loss caused to any individual or organization acting on or refraining from action as a result of the material in this publication can be accepted by the author.

Design and typesetting of text by All In One Book Design.

DEDICATION

I dedicate this book to my parents, Ernie and Elaine Arnow, who always held me to a higher standard. And to my children, Jesse and Haley, who continually soar beyond my wildest expectations. I love you all."

ACKNOWLEDGEMENTS

Jonny Burgess – for inspiring me to dust off my dreams.

Jack Canfield – who's book, *Success Principles*, kicked my blaming, un-responsible victim ass and taught me to set a goal of finishing this book by December 31, 2012.

Jessica Bram and Becky Martin – for being gentle and encouraging when I brought them my first chapters in 2013. And for having the patience to teach me the essentials of writing.

My writing class participants – for listening to the same chapter over and over again without a decrease in enthusiasm.

Maryann Tate – for believing in my book and asking me tough questions which added more meat to my story.

Willa Mitchell – for becoming my partner, blowing belief into me, and spending countless hours rehashing and rereading this book.

My friends and family – for being willing to be themselves in my story and always encouraging me to be my best, courageous self.

Haley Burns – for believing in me and calling me a "cool mom." You are my inspiration.

Jesse Burns – for always making me laugh and being the best son a mom could want.

Table of Contents

Prologue 11
Introduction 15

Part 1 **Awakening**
Chapter 1 Too Old to Look Good 19
Chapter 2 Reunion 21
Chapter 3 The Day after the Reunion 24
Chapter 4 A Seed Was Planted 25
Chapter 5 Breaking My Vow—Return to Weight Watchers 28
Chapter 6 Identity Piece 30
Chapter 7 Did I Blow Another Diet? 31
Chapter 8 Melanie's Story 32

Part 2 **Opening My Eyes**
Chapter 1 I Have No Life 37
Chapter 2 I Should Have Known 38
Chapter 3 Shattered Reality 41
Chapter 4 Getting My Life Back—at the Gym 42
Chapter 5 Starting to Feel like I Matter 44
Chapter 6 Finding Things I Liked to Do 45
Chapter 7 Halloween—I Have No Relationship 46
Chapter 8 Why I Didn't Speak Up/How Had This Happened? 50
　　　　　　The Sensitive Child – a Revelation 52
　　　　　　What Happened? 53
Chapter 9 Promises, Promises 54

Part 3   **Finding the Old Hilary Again**

Chapter 1	The Gym—my Laboratory	61
Chapter 2	Finding an Escape at the Gym	61
Chapter 3	Desiree and Boyfriend	65
Chapter 4	He's Back	70
Chapter 5	Why was I Acting so Goofy?	72
Chapter 6	More Gym Excitement	74
Chapter 7	What do you Wear to the Gym? The Magic Pants!	75
Chapter 8	Wearing the Magic Pants	77
Chapter 9	The Athlete Returns	79
Chapter 10	How could I have Forgotten who I Wwas?	83
Chapter 11	It's Better this Way	85
Chapter 12	Phoenix	86
Chapter 13	Is It Me?	90
Chapter 14	Background on Finances	98
Chapter 15	Steve's Button	102
Chapter 16	Thin Mom, Me?	107

Part 4   **Trouble**

Chapter 1	Who Said It?	111
Chapter 2	Is It In My Head?	112
Chapter 3	Oh, You're On The List	115
Chapter 4	Red Haired Girl	116
Chapter 5	You Made My Day	119
Chapter 6	I'm Your Type?	123
Chapter 7	Hurricane Irene – August 24, 2011	127
Chapter 8	Salve On The Wound	129
Chapter 9	Am I Torn?	134

Chapter 10	Obsessing	139
Chapter 11	He Read the Journal	142
Chapter 12	Why Did You Do This?	147
Chapter 13	Too Dangerous	151
Chapter 14	Go-To Guy	152
Chapter 15	Lovely Lady –	153
	What had Happened to my Marriage?	157
	Could this Work?	148
Chapter 16	Throwing Money at the Problem	157
	Could this Work?	158

Part 5 **Eyes Opening Some More**

Chapter 1	My New Friend	163
Chapter 2	Lunch With The Girls	167
Chapter 3	The Therapist	169

Part 6 **Taking Control of My Life**

Chapter 1	Validation – You Don't Think I'm Crazy?	175
Chapter 2	Triathlon	177
	Part 1: *Just an Idea*	177
	Part 2: *Commitment*	179
	Part 3: *Training*	181
	Part 4: *Race Day*	183
Chapter 3	Jonny And Success Principles	186
	Part 1: *I Used To Have A Dream, Too!!!*	186
	Part 2: *Responsibility*	188
	What Happened To Me?	189
	Part 3: *More About Responsibility*	194
	Part 4: *Purpose*	195

Chapter 4	You're Eating Too Much	199
Chapter 5	Revising My Goals	204
Chapter 6	Women's Empowerment Group	205
Chapter 7	Cracking A Piece Of The Shell	207
Chapter 8	The One Area Not Progressing	213
Chapter 9	Do You Have Time?	215
Chapter 10	Vermont—What Am I Going To Do?	218
Chapter 11	You're Kidding!	222
Chapter 12	One Month Later	223

Epilogue Four Years Later 227

Prologue

Will he be there?

The thought propelled me out of bed. I snuck a peek at my husband of eighteen years as he snored loudly. I moved quietly so as not to wake him. At 4:20 in the morning, I was not in the mood to have another fight.

I slipped on my tight, black exercise pants. My guy friends said they made my butt look good. After removing last night's mascara, I put on enough makeup to look fresh but not overdone. My heart beat fast as I tried to stay calm.

Will he be there? Can I make it another day if he's not?

Ten minutes later I pulled into the fitness club parking lot. I felt like a teenager looking for the guy I had a crush on. I thought my chest would burst as I walked to the back.

Yes! I screamed inside my head. *His bag is here!*

I spotted him on the stair climber. I walked over, grabbed the railings, and hoisted myself onto the machine next to him.

"Hi," he said with his mischievous smile.

He was one of those guys I couldn't help noticing. He walked around the gym with a mesmerizing intensity. He was not handsome in the traditional sense, yet he had a rugged, bad-boy magnetism that was irresistible to my trouble-making side.

About six months earlier, I noticed him on the bike behind me just as I finished on the elliptical. I caught his eye.

"I've been enjoying watching your butt," he said.

"You have?" I asked, surprised, but a tad flirtatious.

"Absolutely," he said. I wandered off with a smile and a dazed look. I added a little more wiggle than usual, hoping he was still enjoying the view.

After that day, we began talking more. In time we started sharing intimate details of our lives. I looked forward to seeing him but was never sure when he would be there. I began arriving every morning at five o'clock, just in case. Missing a day was inconceivable.

This morning there were the sounds of machines swooshing, weights dropping, and people talking in the background, but I was focused only on him. He wore his usual baseball cap that almost covered his sexy, grey eyes. The familiar scent of sweat and cleaning fluid comforted me as we exercised together in silence.

I knew his routine: ten minutes on three different cardio machines. When his stair climber time was done, he said, "Let's go to the bike next."

I followed him to the bikes, thrilled to be invited to spend more time with him. I reveled in our close proximity. He went off to do weights when he finished his cardio. I tracked his moves and anxiously awaited our best time together — stretching. The conversation was private; easier to hear; and less strained by the exertion of exercising.

I kept drifting back to our discussion from the previous day.

"I'm reading a book about pursuing my dreams and goals. What is one of your dreams?" I asked as I squiggled in close to hear his answer.

"Riding a Harley in Santa Barbara, California. I want to get away and relax on the beach."

"Sounds like fun," I said.

My inner voice added, *"and I'm coming with you."*

I enjoyed my thoughts of holding onto his tight body; hair blowing in the wind; laughing together; the vibrations of the Harley....

My daydream was interrupted when I saw him go into the stretching room. I quickly got off my machine and followed.

PROLOGUE

"Mind if I join you?"

I felt the fan blowing on my damp skin as I nervously awaited his answer.

He was on all fours and looked up.

"Not at all," he said. "I was just thinking about California. Cooking up some fresh fish at night for dinner………. So, do you want to come? I was thinking it would be fun to go together. I can picture it...." And he closed his eyes and smiled. He was on his back stretching with his legs up and over his head. It was a perfect view of his tight ass.

I struggled to tear my eyes away. "I would love to come," I said.

I got down on the floor next to him and started stretching.

"Push your legs down closer to your head. Do you feel it in your lower back? So, back to California and the beach, I am loving this idea."

I started to speak but got choked up. He looked at me impatiently, as if to say "What?!" His frustration was palatable until he saw my expression, and then his face softened.

"Thanks for giving me hope," I said, struggling over the lump in my throat. "I didn't want you to go without me."

"Psyched," he said with his beautiful smile. "I've been thinking about it a lot."

"Me, too."

We left the stretching room and walked past the weight machines. I gathered my stuff while he bent down for his bag.

"Go ahead if you're in a hurry," he said.

"No, I like walking out with you," I said. "I hate having to get to the rest of my day."

"Same. You're the only person I can be myself with."

We did his version of a high five, clenched fists, thumb on top, bumping knuckles. "Did I do it right?" I asked teasingly.

"No, but you are getting better," he teased back. "Respect!" he said as he disappeared into the men's locker room. I felt a sense of panic. My body almost followed him in.

FINDING THE OLD HILARY AGAIN

I snapped out of it when I saw the clock on the wall. "Uh-oh," I said and ran like Cinderella to my car, breathing heavily.

I took a second to compose myself and dialed home. "Are the kids up?" I asked my husband.

"Yes," he said. "How was your workout?"

"Fine," I said, trying to sound bored. "I'll be home in ten."

I hung up and sighed. A sense of dread came over me as I started the car. My entire body felt heavy and my head started hurting.

Back to my real life, I thought.

Oh well, there's always tomorrow.

Introduction

I've always believed in fairy tales.

I've always wanted a happy ending.

I got married and thought I was getting mine.

But something happened along the way.

I wasn't even aware of it.

This is my story. There are some things I'm not necessarily proud of, but this is my experience. It's my version of what happened. I have changed some of the names to protect the not so innocent.

And in case writing this book can help someone else, I'm going to tell it.

I hope you are inspired.

If you're someone who judges others, it might be best that you don't read this. The choice is yours. You have been forewarned.

It all began in the mall, the winter of 2009.

PART 1

Awakening

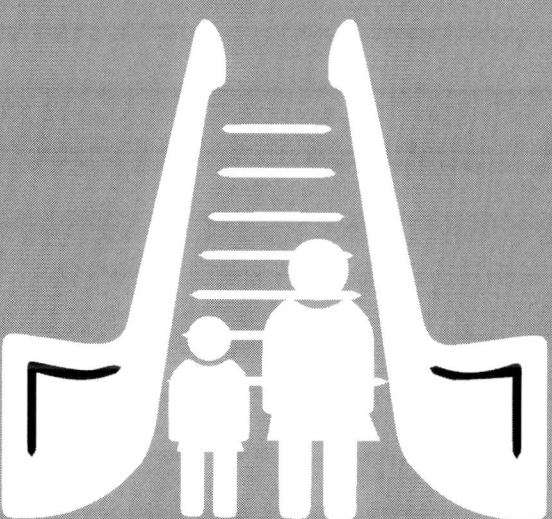

1 Too Old to Look Good

Oh, that poor girl! I thought.

A woman, about my age, late 40s, was descending the escalator across from me. She was overweight, her clothes did nothing for her, and her short haircut reminded me of the pixie I got by mistake in third grade. I stared at her, wondering if she had always looked that way or if she had once looked good.

Had she ever cared about how she looked?

I raised my arm to move my hair out of my eyes. She did, too.

Oh, my God! I thought. *That's me!*

I grabbed the handrail to steady myself, grimacing at the image across the way.

"I am really not looking good," I said out loud without thinking.

"Mom, you're old. You're not supposed to look good," my 11-year-old daughter Haley said matter-of-factly. She bounced off the escalator and headed to her favorite store.

I'm not? Really? Ever again? I asked myself.

I followed Haley in a daze.

I glanced in a mirror.

Was she right?

Was it really too late for me to ever feel good about myself again?

When had this happened? I looked great at my wedding 16 years before.

I went closer to the mirror. My short hair cut was not a good look for my fat face. My leggings were worn, leftovers from my maternity days. I wore my husband's oversized flannel shirt in an attempt to cover the 40 pounds I had never lost after the kids were born.

I told myself I was fine, but the truth was I was ashamed of how I looked.

But what could I do? I had tried every diet known to man. I would lose the weight only to have it come back with a vengeance. I tried praying, making deals with God, and exercising like a maniac.

When that failed, I tried to accept myself as I was.

I would just love myself no matter what my weight was.

But all it took was one glance in the mirror, and the acceptance was replaced with self-loathing. On that day I was still at the top of my weight range.

I followed Haley into the dressing room where, surrounded by mirrors, I was haunted by my image. I felt sick as a memory from 25 years earlier distracted me.

I had moved to Washington, DC, after college. I came back one weekend to see my family in Connecticut. My father and I drove to a local beach to take a walk. It was a beautiful day, and the sound of seagulls overhead was comforting.

We were almost back to the car when my father blurted out, "I am ashamed to look at you. You really look terrible."

I was too shocked to speak. I had only gained five pounds. I just stared at him.

"It's just that I think if you lost weight, guys would be more interested in you, and you wouldn't be as lonely," he continued.

"But dad, what if I lose the weight, meet someone, and then gain it back? Is he not supposed to love me then?"

"Just don't gain it back," he said.

"But what if I do?" I asked, panicked. I kicked a stone out of my way.

"Just don't," was all he would say.

Here I was now, staring at my overweight body, knowing I had gained way more than those five pounds. I put my head in my hands, hardly able to watch Haley trying on clothes. If I could just lose this weight, I knew I could be happy.

So why didn't I just do it? Why was it so hard this time? It's not like I had spent my whole life looking like this.

I thought about it. The times when I struggled with weight were different from the rest of my life—senior years of high school and college, and living in Washington, DC the first couple of years after college. During those three periods, I gained a few pounds and couldn't seem to get them off. Even though it was at most five to ten pounds, I had switched into my alter ego—fat, unworthy, and invisible - and not a person who mattered.

"Just don't," rang in my ears.

I watched Haley try on clothes. I looked in the mirror and stared right into my tear-filled eyes.

But I did, Dad, and now what? Wiping a tear away, I thought, *Is it too late? Can I never look good again?* I quietly whispered, *"I hope not."*

2 Reunion

A few months after the mall incident, our high school class was having a "Turning 50 This Year" reunion. We called it a birthday party for our entire class. I was having trouble turning 50. I felt I could no longer pretend to be young. I was over the half-way mark and felt I now belonged with my parents and older people. It felt like a point of no return.

The months leading up to my birthday had been very uncomfortable. A part of me was happy about seeing my old friends. I wanted to find out if they were having a hard time with

50, like me. But a bigger part of me was terrified. I wanted to hide at home and pretend I still looked like I did in high school.

That day I honored my promise to my classmates and forced myself to drive to the event.

There were about thirty people standing in the back of a white, two-story, antique house. I fought the urge to run back to my car.

They haven't seen me yet. I can still escape, I told myself.

I looked closer at the group and recognized a guy I hadn't seen since we graduated.

"Dave," I screamed, reluctance forgotten. "It's great to see you." I ran to him.

"Hils," he yelled. He grabbed me and hugged me, spinning me around. We held on to each other for a few moments.

"Hils," he said again with a huge smile. "I've missed you. I always tell stories about when we used to hang out together. You were so much fun. Hils!" he exclaimed with love and admiration, grabbing me for a second hug.

I used to be fun? He doesn't even seem to be noticing how bad I look. Amazing.

I walked over to the next group.

"Bob!" I yelled.

"Hils," he said, hugging me. "Thought you weren't going to make it. Oh, group picture. Stand here."

"Renee, Karen, Gina, Amy, Kyle get in," Bob called. We grabbed everyone and helped form a semi-circle.

"Remember the Holly Ball?" I asked Bob. We waited for Greg to snap the picture. I made perverted gestures which made everyone smile widely.

"Yes, but the Senior Prom was even better. Especially the hotel room after," Bob said with a leer.

"You mean the hotel room we shared with 20 people?" I answered, making sure he didn't have a different memory of what had happened.

A warm feeling spread over me.

These people really like me, I thought to myself.

Our arms were linked around each other, and my heart felt like it would burst. We knew each other from growing up together. There were no airs and no need to impress. I didn't have to be someone else. I felt like I had friends.

I felt accepted just as I was. I didn't need to lose weight to feel like I belonged. I had fun and felt happy for the first time in a long time, comforted by an invisible blanket of something wonderful that I couldn't quite explain.

Driving home that night, I started thinking about how I used to be happy…

I remembered myself on my wedding day—thin, shapely body; long blond hair in an up-do; and glamorous, beautiful custom-made gown. I danced for hours, reveling in the moment—family and friends all around me. There were great toasts, and my four brothers and sisters danced to a song they wrote and sang for Jack, my new husband, and me. I was living my dream and inspiring all those in attendance with the love, fun and excitement of that day.

I had high hopes for the future and loved being surrounded by so many loving and wonderful people.

What happened to that fun, dancing, excited Hilary?

I had been telling myself I was living my dream—husband, kids and house—but was I, really?

3 The Day After the Reunion

A bunch of us went to the beach for a softball game the day after the Turning-50-This-Year party. I found myself in the outfield with my old prom date Bob, who I had dated for nine months in junior high. We caught up on each other's families. I was struck by how easy it was to talk with him. He was telling me about his best friend, Greg, who had grown up with us.

"I recommended a book to Greg about a year ago about getting back in shape," Bob said to me. "He read it and took it to heart. Now we go on long bike rides together. He looks great and he feels better, too."

Why is he telling me this? I asked myself. *I work out at least six times a week. Does it not show? I know I'm a little heavy, but I still think I'm in good shape.*

"Are you telling me this for a reason?" I asked.

"No, I just mean it's easy for people to not take as good care of themselves as they get older and too busy. I'm telling you what made a difference for Greg. I remember how athletic you were in high school and how great you looked."

He turned to look me straight in the eyes. "I care about you," he said. He scooped up a ground ball and threw it to first.

Tears welled up, but I gritted my teeth to hold them in.

"I know you're right, and I'm sure my family is horrified by me as well. It's just that I haven't been able to drop this weight," I said, almost choking on my words. "I try to act like it doesn't bother me, but inside I am really ashamed that I look like this." I wiped an escaping tear from my eye, looking away so he wouldn't see.

"Hils, you're always good with me. If you ever need me, just call."

I don't know why I wasn't offended. Maybe because I was used to being criticized about my weight by my parents. I thought I deserved to be condemned on some level for being heavy.

Bob's comments made me feel like he cared. The fact that he was willing to risk our friendship to hold me to a higher standard rekindled a tiny ember of self-pride. He believed in me...even though I had stopped believing in myself.

Our conversation was a wake-up call. Denying I was overweight wasn't working. I got real with myself for the first time in a long time. Rather than continuing to hide under my cloak of resignation and despair, I peeked my head out for just a few minutes. And wondered why it had taken a reunion for me to remember that there were people who knew me, loved me, and were willing to talk straight and tell me what was difficult to hear.

4 A Seed Was Planted

"I lost 70 pounds recently," my college intern said a few weeks after the reunion. My friend Bob's words were still in my head. I couldn't believe she was telling me this. We were sitting in my AFLAC office, where I had started working a few years before.

I turned away from my computer and just stared at her in her size 2 capris. "No way," I said.

"Yes, I did."

I looked her up and down. She was skinny. Not a fat person at all. "There's no way you could have carried 70 more pounds on that little body. How did you lose it?" I asked, still not believing her.

"I counted my points every day using a Weight Watchers calculator. It wasn't that hard. I changed my eating habits and the weight has stayed off for two years."

FINDING THE OLD HILARY AGAIN

Unbelievable, I thought.

I was almost as thin as my intern was now when I graduated from college. I got a job as a systems consultant in Washington, DC and moved there. After a few months, feeling lonely and overworked, I started binge eating at night, just as I had in high school. My roommate was away so there was no one around to judge me. My clothes were getting uncomfortable.

Feeling out of control, I found a local Weight Watchers meeting. I was doing great and losing weight until the third week. The memory of standing in the kitchen eating my absent roommate's frozen home-made chocolate chip cookies horrifies me to this day. I went to my third meeting…anyway.

I was afraid of what I would hear.

"You are up 1.8 pounds," the weigh-in lady said loudly, with a mixture of disdain and glee.

I turned around, publicly humiliated, and walked back to my seat. I sat through the whole meeting with a lump in my throat, holding in tears. When the meeting ended, I ran to my car, burst out crying, and promised I would never be humiliated like that again.

Reliving that 25-year-old embarrassment, I stared at my intern. She really did look great. She only ended up working with me for three days because of the pressure of finals, but she was there long enough to plant a seed. I believe people are in my life for a reason and this was hers.

The next seed was planted at my annual physical. I was sitting on the doctor's bed in a blue dressing gown when my new doctor walked in. I was surprised at her youthful appearance but comforted by her kind manner.

I could smell the antibacterial soap she used to wash her hands. I waited for her to finish reading my chart. She turned and looked at me.

"How is your health overall? Do you have any goals with regards to your weight?"

The last question caught me off guard. I twirled the strings of my dressing gown. I struggled to answer. A strange mixture of panic and relief flowed through me.

"151," popped out of my mouth. "If I could first get to 151, I could get back to my old pre-marriage weight." I said. A tear escaped down my cheek.

"Why that number?" she asked gently, handing me the tissue box.

"It's the number where I got stuck," I said.

After the birth of my son, Jesse, I had dieted and breastfed for six months. I was sure that I had lost all of my "baby weight." I confidently got on the scale, shocked to see I was still up 20 pounds and weighed 151. I stepped on and off about five times, hoping the scale was broken.

After that shocking weigh-in, I gave up on myself and became Fat Hilary again. Rather than continue to lose weight, I slowly gained another 26 pounds over the following fourteen years. I couldn't believe I was now at the weight I was at while pregnant with my first child, Jesse, who was now 14.

I could barely swallow or breathe. I wiped away a tear and just stared at my doctor.

"I don't know what to do anymore," I said. "I've tried everything."

"The best success I've seen is Weight Watchers," she said softly. "Have you ever tried it?"

Of course, it is, I thought to myself. *What do I do now? The second person to bring this up in two weeks. This must be a sign.*

"Yes," I said slowly. "And I think it's time to go back."

5   Breaking My Vow—Return to Weight Watchers

That night, I went online, determined to buy the points calculator that my intern had talked about. I couldn't find it but noticed there was a Weight Watchers meeting in town the very next day. I swallowed my pride and decided to go.

"I am just here to get the calculator," I said to the weigh-in lady. I told her about my experience in Washington, DC.

"We don't announce your weight out loud anymore," she said softly.

"Never?" I asked, eyebrows raised.

"No. Why don't you stay this once?" she asked. "Did you know that people who come to meetings lose 30% more than those who don't?"

Of course, they do. Damn it. Okay, just this once.

I sat in the back and looked around. The leader, Melanie, seemed friendly and down to earth.

"I'm afraid of eating too many carrots," one of the heavier women said.

"Honey, no one is here because they ate too many carrots," another woman blurted out. Everyone laughed.

"Well, I guess you're right. When I compare that to what I could have been eating, that's actually pretty funny." We all giggled and nodded our heads in recognition.

Another woman raised her hand.

"My mother and sister are coming to stay with us. I know they mean well, but I hate when they comment on what I'm eating."

"I had the same problem with my family," Melanie said.

I stopped listening, remembering an incident in my family when I was about eight years old. We were having French toast for breakfast. I reached out to grab a second piece.

"Haven't you had enough?" my mother asked.

I didn't think so, but I pulled my hand back anyway, stunned. I didn't want to embarrass myself any further, so I didn't eat a second piece. It wasn't worth hearing my mother comment. Later that day, we took a walk and window-shopped on our local Main Street. My mother pointed to a very obese woman in front of us and said, "See that lady over there? She had an extra piece of French toast this morning."

I still remember that morning like it was yesterday.

I decided in my eight-year-old mind, that fat people were in a separate category than thin people.

They were there to be ridiculed. In fact, they deserved it.

I might as well have been that woman. Because I HAD wanted that piece of French toast and didn't know I wasn't supposed to eat it.

I stopped trusting myself, thinking my mother knew better than me. I started thinking of myself as a "less than" person who deserved to be insulted.

I took a deep breath.

What if all that wasn't true? Oh, my God, I thought, as the tears started falling. *What if I didn't deserve to be treated poorly? What if I wasn't just "too sensitive" like my mother always said? What if she had just made a really mean comment? What had I been doing to myself all these years?*

The tears were flowing, and I tried not to sob out loud. I wiped my face with my hand. All of a sudden, I looked up. Melanie was standing next to me asking if I was okay.

"Yes," I said, wiping my eyes, "I'm fine." I took the tissues she offered and tried to compose myself for the rest of the meeting.

When it was over, I went to the back and signed up for the monthly pass. It included access to the on-line system and attending weekly meetings.

6 Identity Piece

The next week I was down four pounds.

I was excited. Melanie was pointing to a flip chart. There were circles representing different phases of weight loss.

The final circle was your identity.

"If you lose the weight, but you still think of yourself as fat, guess what will happen?"

"You'll gain the weight back," we all said. She nodded and continued the discussion.

I remembered another incident from childhood that happened when I was eight. I was in bed, and my mother and father came in and sat on my bed. They had never done this before.

"We want you to lose weight," they both said.

"Why?" I asked looking up at them.

"Well, we think you would look better if you were thinner. We will get you a new bicycle if you lose ten pounds."

"I don't know how to do that."

"Stop eating bread and desserts," my mother said.

"Okay," I said obediently. I stopped eating bread and desserts. In a matter of months, I was down the ten pounds and proudly riding my brand-new blue sting ray bicycle. It had a flowered seat and a basket on the handlebars that had bright, colorful plastic flowers.

I could see that I still felt like the little girl on the bicycle who was only okay when she was thin. Fat Hilary needed to be fixed and just wasn't okay. She needed to lose weight in order to get a bicycle.

No wonder I had a hard time asking for what I wanted. I thought I needed to do something to earn it.

Boy did I need to work on this identity piece. I felt like I was in the right place to do it. I was not judged or insulted here. I was safe.

I kept going back.

7 Did I Blow Another Diet?

I was doing well after a month of meetings and was steadily losing weight. One night I was sitting in front of the TV, trying to pay our bills without any luck.

I absently started eating potato chips and chocolate chip cookies. Suddenly, I looked at what was in my hand and panicked. What was I doing? I was eating without thinking.

I've ruined it, I thought.

All my past failed diets went through my head—the grapefruit diet, the ski team diet, the no carb diet, the cleanse, the old Learn to Be Thin program. With all of them, I would start off great then do something wrong. The whole thing was blown. Any weight I had lost would come back, plus a few pounds, and I would end up weighing more than when I started.

What have I done? I thought. *I've ruined it just like all the other times.*

I leaned forward and put my head in my hands. I knew it. I knew I couldn't keep this going. I could feel the tears collecting in the backs of my eyes.

I sat up straight.

Wait. Weight watchers is supposed to be forgiving. Let's see if it actually is.

I ran to the computer and put in all the food I ate. It calculated the points. I couldn't believe it. I had used up the daily points, but then it just put the rest towards my weekly allotment. There were no flashing lights calling me a failure or a loser. No person on the loudspeaker telling me I blew it again and I'd be fat forever.

Wow, I thought. I haven't ruined anything. I am still within the plan. That's incredible. Maybe I CAN do this thing.

I went to that week's meeting and shared my story. I still couldn't believe it. It felt so good to get a little green bravo sticker. I stuck it on my phone and it made me smile every time I looked at it.

8 Melanie's Story

Right before Thanksgiving, our Weight Watchers leader Melanie told us a story that changed my life.

It was Melanie's first year and she was down 40 of the 70 pounds that she eventually lost.

That Thanksgiving, she was calm, knowing she had planned her meal and would be within her points. She had budgeted several glasses of wine. But when she got to her friend's house, instead of four-point wines, her friend was serving 9-point margaritas.

Melanie panicked, knowing she would be way over what she had planned. Feeling like she blew it, she went crazy for the rest of the day, eating and drinking whatever she wanted.

She thought about skipping her next Weight Watchers meeting, but knew if she did, she would probably not return until after New Year's. And could be up 20 pounds by then.

"Even though I was embarrassed to be up seven pounds at the post-Thanksgiving meeting," she said, "it was okay. I got right back on track and the seven pounds were gone by the next week. I continued losing until I was down 70 pounds."

"The lesson I learned is to show up, no matter what."

"Don't quit. Face what you've done, accept it, get back on the program, and keep going. The only way to fail is to quit. Gaining a couple of pounds is just part of the journey."

Her story was instrumental in my weight loss. No matter how bad I thought I did, I made sure I showed up every week. Even when my progress was slow or I hadn't done well, I showed up. Some weeks it was the only good thing I could count on.

When I compared myself to people on other diets, I felt bad seeing their quicker weight losses. But I also saw them stop following their diet and gain the weight back. It made me believe in Weight Watchers.

In the beginning, if I gained or didn't lose, I became negative and very down on myself. I could see that wasn't helping me. Instead I tried to find something positive to focus on. It made me feel much better about my progress.

This time, no matter how badly I wanted to, I didn't quit.

PART 2

Opening My Eyes

1 I Have No Life

After a few months of Weight Watchers, I felt good. I was losing weight in a way that I thought would really work this time. The fact that I was sitting home on another Saturday night didn't bother me, because I wasn't alone—I had Haley, who was now 12, to keep me company. Jesse, my 14-year old son, and Jack were off at Jesse's ice hockey games.

Jack had introduced Jesse to skating when he was just three years old. The next year when Jesse could barely skate, Jack signed him up for hockey lessons. Every year after that, Jack found a team for Jesse to skate on, starting him on the travel team when he was six. We would all spend our weekends at the cold and uncomfortable ice rinks. Not my favorite thing to do, but, seeing as it was the only way the four of us could be together, I went along and brought Haley.

That first year I put up with it, but I couldn't wait for the season to be over. I didn't complain; just patiently waited. Finally, the winter season ended. I was very happy and started planning for us to do other things together. When I saw Jack and Jesse going out the door with their hockey bags the following Saturday morning, I screamed:

"Where in God's name are you going?"

"Spring hockey tryouts," Jack said. They got in the car and drove off.

I sadly realized that hockey season never ends.

2   I Should Have Known

I should have realized that hockey season never ended. Jack had played hockey in college, and I saw on my 35th birthday how much he was still obsessed with it. It was the summer of 1994 and we were engaged. Our wedding was scheduled for August 28th of that year. We attended a friend's wedding on June 10th in the Hamptons. Since they were having a party the next day on June 11th, my birthday, I decided to pretend it was for me too.

Birthdays have always been a big deal to me. As the second of five children, I didn't ask for much. The only time I expected something was on my special day. I looked forward to it all year and made sure everyone knew about it. That year, I was excited to celebrate with Jack and all my friends. We were together, drinking beer and singing songs, and it was exactly how I wanted it to be. I was happy.

Out of nowhere, Jack turned to me and said,

"I'm leaving. I have a toothache."

"Wait," I said. "What do you mean?"

"I'm leaving," he said and turned around towards the door.

"But how am I going to get home?" I asked his back as he walked out the door without answering.

I stayed behind and tried to continue my fun, but I was no longer in the mood. I couldn't understand how Jack could just walk out. My friends were used to me being fun, and they pressured me to go out with them after the party. I just couldn't. My birthday was ruined. I asked around until I found someone who could give me a ride. I wanted to see if Jack was okay. For him to leave like that, he must not have felt well at all.

I walked into the house, ready to be Florence Nightingale and nurse him back to health. I was shocked to see him happily sitting in front of the TV, drinking beer and watching the Stanley Cup finals, toothache forgotten.

"Are you kidding me?" I said loudly. "Since when does hockey season go into June? I thought it was a winter sport." Jack ignored me and mumbled something about the Rangers being in the Stanley Cup finals.

Looking back, it's hard to imagine that I didn't say something.

I think I didn't want to be a complaining, high-maintenance fiancée. I had seen women who complained, and they had husbands who rolled their eyes. I didn't want to be one of those horrible, annoying women. Instead, I figured I was just being sensitive and asking for too much. I joined Jack on the couch and numbed my disappointment with another beer.

In the following days, I questioned my feelings and invalidated them rather than saying anything. How could I complain? The Rangers hadn't won the Stanley Cup in 50 years. And Jack did end up with an emergency root canal.

Did a 35-year old woman really need to be fussed over on her birthday? Maybe it was time to grow up.

But as the years went by, it got harder and harder to keep quiet. My annoyance with hockey grew.

"When are we going to do something together like normal people?" I would periodically ask.

"Let's see...tonight. The Sound Tigers are playing home tonight. Let's go to the game. Some of my old hockey buddies will be there." It was always hockey. If Jesse didn't have a game, and there wasn't a local professional hockey game to watch, there was always some kind of hockey game on TV.

The years went by.

Haley and I gradually stopped going to hockey with the boys.

When Jack's law practice was losing its main client and our income was dropping, I started resenting the money and time Jack was putting into Jesse's hockey. Rather than build up new clientele, Jack put all his attention on our 10-year old son's hockey career. My bitterness and financial insecurity grew.

"When is this going to end?" I asked from time to time.

"Not any time soon," Jack said. "Why are you complaining? I could be doing something much worse like womanizing, drugging or gambling. How could you deny me this time with my son, a devoted father helping his son pursue his dream?"

"Most women would be happy to have a man like me."

I started questioning myself.

Would other women be happy?
Was I asking for too much?
Was I just an ungrateful bitch?

I ignored my feelings. Nothing I said changed anything. My husband would not deny Jesse anything related to hockey. I just shut down and became a silent victim, questioning my wants, thoughts and opinions. Jack was a lawyer.

He was very good at making me think he was right.

It seemed like there was nothing I could say to change things. Jack did what he wanted to do. I continued to pretend nothing was wrong. On Fridays when hockey began for the weekend, I numbed my discomfort with food and alcohol. Pretty soon, I thought my only problem was my weight. It had an easier solution and was something I knew how to fix.

I didn't know how to make Jack behave differently.

Over time, I stopped being sad when the boys left and looked forward to it. Haley and I had the house to ourselves. She was my buddy. We stayed home so we wouldn't spend money, and we still had a good time. Since Jesse was Jack's, I considered Haley to be mine. I thanked

God I had her. I gave up trying to have an influence over Jesse. Jack took over Jesse's hockey and life. Jesse, who was like me in not liking conflict, didn't speak up and just went along with what Jack wanted.

3 Shattered Reality

My reality was shattered one Saturday evening. I had planned on spending the night watching movies with Haley like we always did. I was looking through the channels when Haley tapped me on the shoulder.

"Mom, can you take me over to Emma's house?" she asked, bouncing up and down.

"Why?" I asked trying to remain calm.

"Her parents just said she could have some kids over."

"Sure," I said trying to sound like I was okay with it. She ran upstairs to get ready.

I drove her there and came back to an empty house. The lyric to the Sam Cooke song "It's Saturday Night and I Ain't Got Nobody" kept playing over and over in my head.

I went into the kitchen to fix my dinner and started thinking about my life. Haley had her own plans and her own friends. That was a good thing. So why did I feel so abandoned? What was wrong with me? How pathetic was it that my social life revolved around my 12-year old?

I cleaned the lettuce for my salad.

I had put my family first for 14 years. I never made plans for myself in case they needed me. How stupid. Not only did they not need me, but it seemed that they really didn't give a shit about me at all.

I sat at our rickety snack table in front of the TV. It seemed like other mothers had their own lives. Nobody else was sitting home by themselves trying not to spend money. What was wrong with me?

I obviously didn't need to stay home anymore in case the kids needed me.

It was time to make my own life and have my own interests. I could start with the things I used to enjoy doing.

Was this selfish? I wondered.
Was it wrong of me to want something different?
Was that being a bad mother?
Or was I finally getting smart?
If my family needs me, they can ask me for my time, I decided. *It was time to start having a life of my own.*

4 Getting My Life Back—at the Gym

The next day, buoyed up my new resolve, I decided to make some changes.

Since I was at the gym anyway, it was an easy place to start. For years I had been doing the same thing every day: 65 minutes on the same elliptical, hiding in the corner, and not talking to anybody.

I caught myself heading to my usual machine. Instead, I forced myself to try a different kind of elliptical in the middle of the room. I got on and started moving my legs back and forth. It wasn't natural at first, but I got it going after a couple of minutes. I couldn't help looking back at my old hiding place. I could almost see my pre-Weight-Watchers self in worn black stretch pants and oversized sleep shirt, reading for 65 minutes and then leaving…

Now, in the middle of the cardio section, I watched *Good Morning America* featuring the *Dancing with the Stars* couple who had been eliminated the night before. I found myself laughing as the dancers joked and talked with the hosts. I felt eyes staring at me and glanced up.

"Hi!" a very tall man said.

"I couldn't help noticing your smile."

He held out his hand. "I'm Scott."

My smile? Me?

I looked up at him again. He looked friendly. My friends might have acted rude thinking this was a pick-up line, but I was thrilled that someone was noticing me at all. I remembered I used to like being friendly to people.

"I'm Hilary," I said, shaking his large hand. I couldn't help wondering if he shopped in a Big and Tall store.

"I don't know why I haven't seen you before," he said.

"I've kind of been hiding…And doing my weights at home."

I told him I was ready to branch out and do the weights in public again. He encouraged me to get my free training session even though I had had one five years before.

I scheduled and went to my free session and learned enough to get started. I felt self-conscious at first. I couldn't always remember the exact way to do something, but I learned to ask the guys for help. Most of them were more than willing to assist. As the weight came off, I took off the baggy clothes and started caring about what I wore. I started wearing a little makeup, too.

5 Starting To Feel Like I Matter

A couple of weeks later, I was doing weights on the main floor of the gym and I spotted Ernie.

Ernie and I had worked together in high school at the local movie theater. We had also connected briefly when I lived in New York City. He had a great sense of humor and I always felt better after seeing him.

"Ernie," I yelled.

He was using the arm machines and stopped mid-lift when he saw me.

"Whoa," he said. "What are you doing? You are looking good."

"Really," I said. "You can tell?" I spun around, aware of how my new black capri pants hugged my slowly shrinking butt. They weren't tight, but it was a far cry from how I used to look. My maroon t-shirt actually stopped at the waist.

"Seriously, you can tell?" I repeated, eager to elicit a compliment.

"Turn around again," he said. "Oh yeah. You are getting back to your old self."

"I am very proud of you."

"Thanks, Ern," I said, grabbing him in a hug. I didn't want to let go, embarrassed that my eyes were welling up.

"You made my day," I said.

I walked off feeling like a new person. It had been so long since I had gotten a compliment. I was happy that my hard work was paying off and that somebody noticed.

I stopped being the obese woman walking down the street and started being someone who mattered again.

Invisible Hilary was still on the elliptical in the corner, dressed in her old maternity clothes.

New Hilary started walking differently and strutting just a little bit.

6 Finding Things I Liked to Do

A few days later after I finished my weights, Big and Tall Scott was standing outside one of the exercise rooms. There were women inside dancing to the music. It was Zumba.

I pointed to the room. "That looks like fun."

"Why don't you do it?"

"Because they all know what they're doing. I'm kind of intimidated."

"I thought you told me you were out of hiding," Scott said.

I looked at him, biting my lip.

"You'll feel better if you conquer your fears."

"Go for it."

He gave me a gentle nudge in that direction. "And keep smiling."

I walked into the room slowly and joined the class. I tried to follow the moves and avoided looking in the mirror. As long as I couldn't see myself, I could pretend that I didn't look that bad.

Over the course of several weeks, I found different Zumba classes to go to. I imitated the other women's suggestive moves—gyrating, shimmying and thrusting my hips. I started getting a little better and started feeling sexy for the first time in many years.

One day I was practicing moving my hips in a circular movement while keeping to the beat. I couldn't help grinning when I felt like I was doing it right.

I looked around me. We were a bunch of women having a good time. There were no men involved—just us. I felt like I had been let into a secret. I wasn't dependent on a man to make me happy.

What a novel concept, I thought, shaking my butt back and forth faster than I ever had before.

Another day I was practicing my shimmy, moving my hips around in a circle, and I remembered that I had always loved good music and dancing – cheerleading in high school, aerobics classes, and rock and roll clubs when I lived in New York City. It always brought joy to my life.

Wow, I thought. *I don't think I've been this happy since my 50th birthday reunion.*

It felt great. Gone were the days of sitting around in case my family needed me. I was determined to be more selfish and enjoy myself more often. This was fun.

I walked out of the gym that day smiling, proud and, most importantly, filled with hope. I was doing what I said I would do— finding things that I enjoyed doing, having fun, and feeling good about myself again.

7 Halloween—I Have No Relationship

It was Halloween night, 2010. At 14 years old, Jesse was already out with his friends. Figuring I'd be taking Haley and her friends out, I started thinking about which shoes would be the most comfortable to walk in. I was looking forward to sharing the excitement of the evening, as well as her candy!

Uh oh, I thought as I sat on the couch in my living room.

I remembered a pre-weight watchers Halloween where I went crazy. I had eaten a bunch of snickers, peanut M&M's, Reese's peanut butter cups, and Butterfingers and gained three pounds.

I have a choice, I thought.

Go crazy and pay for it at Tuesday's weigh-in or figure out how many points I have to spare and plan for it.

"Mom, can you take me to Hannah's?"

I pulled my head out of my candy trance. "What?"

"Hannah's mother said she would take us trick or treating around their street."

I just stared at her.

I had assumed I was taking her out around here like last year.

I took a deep breath.

Time to let go. She's now in middle school. My baby was growing up.

"Sure," I said with a sigh.

We arranged that I would drive her there and our neighbors would drive her home. It dawned on me that both kids had plans out of the house. This hadn't happened since Jesse was born 14 years before. My mind started spinning.

"Hey Jack," I said excitedly. "We're going to be alone tonight. What should we do?"

He was busy on the computer and kind of mumbled something. As I drove Haley, I allowed myself to fantasize about the kind of night I had always wanted. I pictured candles, wine, soft music, and wonderful intimacy. Reality did not enter my mind. It had been so long since we had been alone together that it was easy to blame our lack of romance on the kids, instead of remembering that Jack had never actually been that way.

That Halloween night, my fantasy mind took over. On the drive home, I created a wonderfully romantic, loving sexual evening with Jack in my mind. It never occurred to me it wasn't real. I had convinced myself that it was—or would be.

I sang *Oh, What a Night* to the radio. I could barely wait to get home.

I walked into the house with anticipation. Jack was still on the computer.

Well, that's ok, I thought, giving him the benefit of the doubt. *I'm sure he'll be finished soon.*

I didn't let it affect my attitude. I was determined to have a good night. I went into the kitchen to pour myself a glass of wine. I sat down in front of the TV.

"Are you watching this?" I asked, in an effort to have him notice me and turn off the hockey game.

"Yes," he said. "It's a great game, the Rangers and the Islanders. I am loving it."

"Oh," I said dejectedly. I went to get my book. Great.

I grabbed a couple of pillows and put them behind my back, trying not to notice the worn sofa, stains on our chairs, and the marks on the walls.

Don't go there, I thought.

I picked up my book, trying to stay upbeat in anticipation of the night to come.

Hmmm, I thought.

I looked up a half-hour later to see Jack still huddled over his computer. His back was hunched in concentration as he hunted and pecked on the keyboard. I watched him, curious to see if he would look up. He finally did.

"Oh my God, did you see that?" He jumped out of his seat and came towards me. I got excited and started to make room for him on the couch. He stood, watched the rerun, commented loudly on the goalie's missed shot, and returned to his chair at his computer. He put his head back down and started typing again.

Not allowing myself to feel the disappointment, I went for the chips and hummus.

Fuck it, I thought. *I might as well enjoy myself. Food was my old friend.*

I set up one of our old white snack tables, trying to ignore the chipped paint and rickety legs, and set myself up for a feast.

What the hell, I thought and brought out the wine bottle, as well.

With each chip I dipped and ate, I sank lower into the couch, hunching over the food. As I poured more wine, my upper cheekbones tingled, and my back tensed. I continued to berate myself until the remaining bag of chips, hummus and wine were gone. Full, drunk and disillusioned, I gave up.

I put the food away and started upstairs.

"Can you pick up the kids if they call?" I asked over my shoulder, trying to sound normal.

"Sure," he said, barely looking up.

I went upstairs. As I brushed my teeth, I looked in the mirror and noticed more wrinkles, puffiness around my eyes, and new sun-damage spots. I got into bed and lay there, finally letting myself feel the unbearable sadness and loneliness.

My marriage was a disappointment. I couldn't pretend anymore that it wasn't. Numbing the pain was no longer working. It felt like I was being stabbed in the heart, and a piece of it broke off that night. By focusing on my kids and weight gain instead of my marriage, I had hidden what was lacking between us. That night shined a light on it that was too bright to ignore.

I tossed and turned. I made a decision.

I needed to do something.

I had tried to talk to Jack, but he didn't seem to care. I didn't want to keep using food and alcohol to pretend that everything was fine. I was good at pretending, but it was costing me my soul and vitality. I did not sign up for misery on our wedding day. I was tired of feeling bad.

8 Why I Didn't Speak Up/How Had This Happened?

Why had I not just asked Jack for what I wanted? What if I had just asked him to pay attention to me? He might have said yes and my whole story would have ended up differently.

Easy to say now, but at that time it wasn't an option. I thought that if Jack wanted to spend time with me, he would. Why should I have to ask him? How pathetic was that? And I didn't think I could take it if he STILL ignored me. It was easier to withdraw and protect myself than risk additional rejection.

As time has passed, I have started understanding a little about why I didn't speak up. I've started noticing patterns that I developed in childhood.

In studying ontology, this is what I learned. When babies are born, they are fully self-expressed and unconstrained. All is well, life is great. Then something happens and their subconscious mind makes assumptions about life. The child doesn't know these assumptions are made; life is just different. The amygdala, a part of the brain, has a job – develop strategies to keep the child safe.

"Don't do that, don't speak up, don't touch that hot stove." Some of the strategies are helpful, but others are limiting. We are not aware of these new filters. They become our blind spots.

My blind spots can only be explained by telling you about my "driveway incident."

Here's how it goes: I was little, about 2 or 3 when the neighbors I'll call the Smiths, still lived next door. Life was great. My sister, Sherry, and I loved Tom Glaser, a folk singer who was famous in the early 1960's. We sang his songs all day long – On top of Spaghetti, sung to the tune of On Top of Old Smokey was our favorite song.

I knew my neighbors had gotten tickets to a Tom Glaser concert. I assumed I was going and was really, really, really excited.

My sister and I went out to their driveway to get into the Smith's car. Sherry got in. When I tried to get in, they told me to wait in the driveway. They were just going around the corner for milk. I waited.

When they got back, I started getting in the car. "What are you doing?" my sister asked.

"Going to the concert," I said, still ignorant and excited.

"We already went," she said, pushing me out of the way. Sherry and her friend happily burst out of the car, singing my favorite song.

I stood there, stunned, not realizing what had happened. When I finally figured it out, I ran into my house, sobbing unconsolably. My mother, probably busy with my newborn brother, told me to stop crying.

"Don't be upset," she said. "Nothing's worth getting that upset over. Stop it. Don't be upset."

In retrospect, she was busy. There was nothing she could do.

But in my little girl mind, something was now wrong. Why didn't they take me? What was the matter with me? Why did she lie? Why couldn't I go? Why didn't my mother understand why I was upset? Why did she keep telling me to stop crying?

The world changed for my little girl self. I could no longer trust people. I couldn't have what I wanted. No one understood. I didn't know what I had done. No one would tell me what happened. I was powerless.

And, worst of all. I was upset. And I wasn't supposed to be. And after many other times when I was upset and was told, "you shouldn't be, you're just too sensitive," I really thought there was something wrong with me.

I learned to pretend I wasn't. I became "fine". I turned the blame onto myself. It was *my fault* if I was upset. I couldn't be my "real" self, so I became who my mother wanted me to be. I didn't want to lose her love.

The same thing if I was disappointed. If I was, it was my fault. I'd tell myself I shouldn't have gotten my hopes up like I did for Tom Glaser. Don't expect anything and you won't be disappointed. "People lie and there's nothing you can do about it."

"I must be stupid for expecting something," I'd say to myself. Rather than feel the disappointment or speak up, I would berate myself and turn the problem on me.

And I became good. And quiet. And accepted the normal critical nature of our growing up life. It was mine to endure. "I'm just too sensitive." I shouldn't be hurt by the things people say. I should just "get over it."

THE SENSITIVE CHILD – A REVELATION

Being a sensitive child was something I was ashamed of and tried to hide all my life. I thought it was a defect I was born with.

Recently though, I learned something that had me question my thinking. According to Webster, "some children are more easily hurt or damaged, especially easily hurt emotionally. They can be delicately aware of the attitudes and feelings of others."

Unlike what I had been told, being sensitive is not a problem. It can even be a gift. Empathy and the ability to love and feel deeply can be the positive traits of sensitivity, something that less sensitive people may not be able to do.

According to one doctor who is studying addictions, to a sensitive child, being told not to be something is life altering at that age. A child needs his mother's love to survive. If he is told not to be upset, mad, violent or anything, he learns to adapt in order to maintain the mother/child attachment. But in the process, he loses his ability to be authentic or himself. In my case, I decided I couldn't be loved if I was upset or disappointed.

This doctor asserts that sensitive children can develop addictions because of their inability to be authentic. They don't know what's wrong, but they feel that something is missing. They can't really be happy because they think they can't be loved as they are.

When they find something that can numb this pain, they feel free. It feels euphoric. The pain and suffering disappear, and they are finally ok. They don't want this feeling to end; so, they keep numbing themselves.

In my case, I can now understand why I developed a couple of ways to numb myself.

As a younger child, I created a fantasy life. It was the early 60's and Sherry and I had pictures of the four Beatles on our bedroom wall. Paul McCartney became my secret friend. I talked to him silently in my head. I could be myself with him. He loved me unconditionally. I could be anyway I wanted to be. He wouldn't leave me in the driveway. I was happy.

As I got older, food became another way to numb myself. Because my eating was closely monitored by my parents, as a teenager, I learned to "sneak eat". For me it was a rebellious act, getting a buzz when I got away with it. I now realize I was only hurting myself.

WHAT HAPPENED?

When Jack and I got married, I was in a great place—I had done the Landmark Forum and had started speaking up - my weight was good, my hair was good, I was successful in my job and made great money. I had friends. I had fun, exercised, and had confidence. I felt powerful and was ready to have an extraordinary adventure with the man I married.

Jack was great when we were dating. When I was upset, he was understanding and wonderful. I called him my "best friend" and that I "could tell him anything." I was looking forward to my future with him. I was confident that any issues could be resolved in communication. I was sure that I had found someone like Paul McCartney, but in real life. Jack seemed to love me just as I was. I was happy.

Shortly into the marriage, something changed. He didn't act like a friend at all and didn't have time to listen. I felt like I was bothering him if I tried to tell him anything.

I would try to talk to him at the door when he was leaving for work.

"Call me, I have to go."

But when I called him, he was busy.

Later it got worse. If I was upset, he was disgusted.

"You are the most upset person I know. Do you know that you are always upset?"

Looking back at that time, I can see that my old driveway pattern took over. I blamed and questioned myself for being upset and lost my confidence.

My common thoughts were: "Don't be upset. It's your fault. You shouldn't have expected so much from your marriage. Your expectations were just too high. This is real life. Get used to it. Life is not a romance novel."

At that time, I didn't know I had reverted to my old patterns. I did the best thing I knew to do: protect myself. And went to bed without saying anything to Jack.

9 Promises, Promises

The next morning, I went to the gym. I pushed myself past the point of comfort and watched my heart rate soar. I did a quick 45 minutes and drove home stone-faced as I tried to make sense of the night before.

I got home in time to get the kids ready for the bus. I showered, dressed, and carefully avoided Jack. I headed to my regular Dunkin' Donuts, anticipating the comfort of my morning coffee.

Damn it, I thought.

There he was in the parking lot, looking like a sullen stalker. I decided to forgo my caffeine addiction and started backing up my car.

"Wait!" I heard him yell.

"What?" I snarled.

"Why are you avoiding me?'"

"Gee, let's see. Did *you* have a good time last night?" I asked sarcastically.

"Yes," he said smiling. "I typed the letter I was working on and watched the hockey game. I enjoyed it. The Rangers won in overtime. Why do you ask?"

"It was the worst night of my life, second only to my 35th birthday fiasco. This marriage is over. I am done."

"What?" he said shocked. "What do you mean? What happened? We were together all night."

"Together? You call that together? You didn't talk to me once. You didn't even know I was there."

"I thought you were having a good time. You were sitting there reading. Why didn't you say something?"

"I was too upset. I couldn't even talk. You didn't even notice that I was in the same room. I am done. I can't do this anymore."

"W-w-what are you talking about?" he stuttered when he was upset. "W-w-what can I do?"

By now, we were inside. The men in the line at Dunkin' Donuts looked at him with a combination of pity and understanding as he tried to get the words out. We were sitting at a high table by the door, so it was difficult not to hear us.

"Nothing. It's too late." I got up to go. I had my hand on the door handle, cringing as I grasped the sticky knob.

"Please," he cried out. "Don't go yet. What can I do? Tell me what's not working, and I will change. I will do anything."

He looked so pathetic and lost that somewhere deep inside I found my anger melting.

My compassionate nature ignited a small sliver of hope while I watched him squirm and beg.

I stared at him, thinking. "Let me get my coffee first."

I rose to get my large French vanilla with skim and went back to the table.

"Get out a piece of paper. I will give you a list of things that need to change or I am out." He ripped a piece of paper from his notebook and took a pen from his jacket pocket.

"Start writing." I dictated as he wrote carefully and methodically in his block capital letters.

"PAY ATTENTION TO ME."
"LISTEN AND DON'T ARGUE."
"SAVE MONEY, AND NO CREDIT CARDS."
"SEX/PHYSICAL TOUCH."
"GO OUT LIKE NORMAL COUPLES."
"DO WHAT YOU SAY YOU WILL DO."

"That's a start," I said.

"Ok," he said anxiously. "I will do these. Will you give me another chance?"

"Sure," I said timidly. A part of me wimped out. Inside, a voice was screaming at me not to give in.

But he really means it this time, I argued silently. *Maybe this happened for a reason. He really seems like he wants to change. Maybe it can be like I've always wanted it to be We'll see,* the voice said.

As the days went by, I anxiously awaited this attention. Sadly, nothing changed. He still was on his computer, going out to hockey at night and on the weekends, and definitely no sex.

My hope shrank as again, I realized I had fallen for his empty promises.

A few weeks later I was in his car looking for something, and there on the floor was "the list that was to save our marriage", crumpled up and dirty, obviously forgotten. The last ember of hope was doused as my heart ripped a little bit more.

The voice in my head went crazy. *I knew it. You fell for it again. Will you ever learn? You know better than to get your hopes up*

Yes, I answered myself. *I may be dumb, but I'm not stupid. I don't know how yet, but I'm not going to fall for it again. I am determined that things are going to change and I'm starting right now.*

PART 3

Finding the Old Hilary Again

1 The Gym—my Laboratory

I needed to feel good again. The gym continued to be my laboratory. I branched out on the main floor doing weights. It was a whole new world out there. I couldn't help but interact with people. It was different than when I hid in the corner.

After seeing the same people every day, I started smiling and saying hello.

"Are you using this?" was easy to ask. "Do you know how to use this machine?" "Are you working your biceps?" were all questions that felt natural.

I found myself smiling at people and starting to feel like I had a community. I knew people, and when I walked through the gym, it felt like high school. I had friends who liked me, who talked to me, and who made me feel like a regular person.

I felt comfortable moving through the various sections of the gym—cardio, stretching area, weights, and abs. I was happy, waving to people and having them smile and wave back. I felt relevant, and that I belonged.

It started feeling like a different world than home. I was carefree and only focused on my workout. Husband, children, money problems, and stress all disappeared. I was there to exercise and have fun. I mattered. Being at the gym was the highlight of my day.

2 Finding an Escape at the Gym

Within a few months I was doing weights every other day. One day, I was facing the mirrors, lifting weights to strengthen my arm muscles, when I felt someone watching me, again. I looked up and caught the eyes of a guy using one of the nautilus machines behind me.

A surge of excitement flowed up my arms when I realized it was the cute guy I had noticed a few weeks before. He finished what he was doing and got up. My eyes followed the outline of his butt until he rounded the corner out of view. My ears and head were now tingling as I paused to catch my breath. I didn't even know his name.

As the weeks went by, I felt extra motivation to come much earlier than I had been every day. I looked forward to catching glimpses of this guy. Once I knew which color he was wearing, it was easier to track him as he moved around the gym.

One weekend, Jack and Jesse were away at a hockey tournament. I walked into the gym Friday morning, deciding I needed to feel good about something. Before the weekend was over, I was going to be bold enough to find out the cute guy's name.

I waited two days for an opportunity to talk to him. Finally, from my perch on the elliptical, my heart racing, I watched him walk past me and get on the machine behind me. Quickly, I grabbed my book, towel and water and climbed onto the machine next to him before I could chicken out.

"Hi." I said. "How do you like this machine? I am used to the ones with arms."

That was dumb, I thought.

"It's fine. I just do 15 minutes and I'm done."

"I heard you can increase your metabolism by getting your heart rate up," I said. I put my two fingers to the pulse in my neck. My Weight Watchers leader told me that I was probably used to doing the elliptical. She suggested doing it for less time but getting my heart rate up. For the last couple of weeks, I had been able to get my heart rate up over 130. I started counting the beats to see if I was in the right range.

"You don't have to do that." he said laughing. "The machine will calculate it for you. Watch." He showed me how to use the sensors to have the machine calculate it for me.

I tried it and watched the numbers crawl up almost to my cardio zone. "It's so much easier this way. Thanks. I'm Hilary, by the way," and I stuck out my hand.

"Tom," he said.

I had seen him leave around 8:30 every morning wearing jeans, and I figured him for a blue-collar worker with a truck. His smile was adorable, and his blue eyes looked great with his silver-grey hair. I decided to be even bolder. "Where do you work?" I asked.

"I am retired from Xerox after working there for 30 years," he answered. "I was offered a package and a lifetime pension. I'm happy to be done working, set financially, and able to enjoy my life. Well, nice to meet you, Hilary, I'm off to do abs." he said. He got down and walked off.

I felt a thrill that he remembered my name as I watched his butt walk off into the other gym section.

Lifetime pension and retired? Not bad, I thought.

I sighed. I would love to be with a man like that.

I felt a rush of adrenalin. I realized I had gotten his name. I made it happen even though I was nervous. It felt great going outside my comfort zone. Maybe I had some of my old ballsy personality left, after all? YAY ME! Maybe there was some life left in this old girl. I smiled for the whole weekend.

A few days later, I was walking past the men's locker room door at the gym. Tom was talking to some friends.

"Wait up," he said after excusing himself from the conversation to follow me. "I told you all about me. Where do you work?" he asked.

His eyes looked even bluer than the last time. He looked like he was posing—one knee up on the part of the wall that came to thigh height. His arms were folded, and he was cocking his head toward me. His expression was one of interest.

I just stared at him for a second.

He wanted to know about me?

I shook my head, trying to clear it to be able to focus on his question.

"I work for AFLAC," I quacked. "I am a district sales manager for them."

"I love the duck. Do you like it?" he asked. The euphoria surging through me like a drug was making it difficult to think.

When was the last time a cute guy wanted to know about me?

"I like parts of it, um-mm…"

Focus, I yelled at myself silently.

"I like the people part."

We continued to talk about the difficulties of being on commission and how he knew he had to "sell to eat." He loved the excitement but was glad to be retired.

I was facing the exercise rooms as I talked, smiling widely and feeling a giddiness in my upper body.

Oh shit, I thought.

Jack was walking towards me.

He rarely comes to the gym. Why today of all days?

I quickly considered pretending I didn't see him. He caught my eye.

Damn it.

I took a deep breath.

"Jack, meet Tom. Tom, this is my husband, Jack." I told him about Tom's past in commission sales. "Jack works with me at AFLAC."

"Oh, hi," Tom said. "My wife also works in sales, but she has not retired yet." Jack and Tom started talking.

The elation I had felt was replaced with annoyance. Why did Jack have to show up and ruin my big moment? I hated that I had to introduce him. And, why did Tom having a wife bother me so much?

"It was nice talking to you," I said softly, walking towards my comfortable old elliptical in the corner.

I watched Jack and Tom continue their chat and my annoyance grew. I left that morning wondering what was happening to me.

3   Desiree and Boyfriend

A few weeks after the Halloween incident, I was sitting at Desiree's hair salon waiting to get my hair cut and colored. I had been to Desiree a few times already and knew she ran late, but this was ridiculous. I had already waited two hours and she was nowhere near ready for me.

I sat on the leather couch thumbing through magazines, wondering why I was putting up with this. I asked the woman next to me if it bothered her.

"No, I'm used to it. I just figure I'll be here all night. It's my time away from my family. I catch up on my magazines, relax, and get pampered."

I'm not sure if I can do this, I thought.

I crossed and uncrossed my legs trying to get comfortable.

If I leave, I have to find someone else to cut and color my hair. The last four people either chopped off my hair or left it in a mullet—top short, bottom long so I either looked masculine or like a 60's male rock star. Not attractive. At least Desiree listened to me. When I went to Desiree the second time, she told me to go away.

"It can't grow if you keep cutting it."

"But I hate it."

"Too bad. I'm going to help you feel good about yourself again. Trust me. You have nice hair, a good face, and will be easy to work with."

And she had. My face was getting thinner and my hair was getting longer. She helped me cover the grey strands at my hairline. She even shaped and dyed my eyebrows, something that I never thought of doing. I was starting to feel a little more feminine and attractive.

Tonight, though, instead of feeling love and gratitude, I was annoyed. There was still one person in her chair, and it was already 9:30 PM. "I have to go. I'll come back another time," I said, standing up and putting my coat on.

"Relax. I'll be right with you. Why don't we open up this bottle of white wine?"

That's what she said an hour ago, I thought.

My back hurt and I had a headache. What should I do? Could I relax? I sighed and went out to the car to get my book. I started reading and grabbed the plastic cup of warm wine. Each time I looked at the clock, my headache came back.

My friends would never put up with this, I thought.

I looked in the mirror at my roots. But if I didn't do it that night, I didn't know when I could do it.

OK, I'll stay this time, but I may not come back.

I took a deep breath and re-opened my book.

Finally, at 10:05 PM she started mixing my color.

"So how is everything?" Desiree asked, when the prior customer had walked out the door. We were on our second bottle of wine.

Tears suddenly filled my eyes. I watched them drip onto the plastic cape as I sat in the salon chair. I stared at myself in the mirror, unable to speak over the now familiar lump in my throat.

"What's going on?" Desiree asked.

I took another long slug of wine. Where to begin? I hadn't told anyone about my marriage, especially what had happened on Halloween. Who talked about those things? The stress of waiting all evening, plus the wine, must have loosened my tongue and my self-control.

"My marriage sucks," I blurted out.

"Why? I've met Jack and it always seems like you guys get along pretty well."

I squinted my eyes closed and pressed my lips together. I erupted into full body sobbing. "We have no physical relationship. We don't even touch each other," I said.

"You mean you don't have sex? How can that be?" she asked, her eyes bugging out.

I struggled to take in air. I wheezed in between sobs. "It's been years. He says I am not his type and it doesn't occur to him to have sex with me."

"What do you mean you're not his type? Why did he marry you then?"

"Well, he says it was for other reasons. We were good friends and could talk about anything back then. It seemed like we wanted the same things."

"Was it always this way sexually? Do you think it was because you gained weight?" she asked.

"No, even when I was thin it was never great, but at least we tried. After a while, he kept putting me off until I finally had enough rejection and stopped bringing it up. Now we just don't do anything."

"Do you think he's having an affair? Do you think he has someone on the side?"

"No, I don't think so. He just has no interest in it, he says. I know it's my fault, but…."

"What?" Desiree screamed. "Oh, honey, why would you think it is your fault? This is SO not your fault."

I looked at her image above mine in the mirror, tears still streaming down my face.

"I just figured there was something wrong with me. Why else would he not want it?"

"This is *SO* not you. There is something wrong with Jack. Guys like sex. They don't say no to sex," she said as she changed scissors. "Watch this."

"Michael, have you ever said no to sex," she asked her boyfriend who was across the room folding towels.

"Never," he said with a lecherous smile. "Nope, never. Not once."

"See," she said. "This is *SO* not your fault. It's him. It isn't natural for a guy to turn down sex."

"Really?" I asked. "Are you sure?"

"Yes," she said. "You are looking good and you are kind and fun and smart. You are fine."

I cried harder. All this time, I thought I was so undesirable that my husband didn't even want to have sex with me. The pressure in my chest felt like I was suffocating. I squinted my eyes shut and blew out some air. I cried silently, letting myself feel the pain and shame that I had buried deep inside me for so long. I felt like I was being stabbed in my upper abdomen.

What if it actually wasn't me? What if it WAS Jack, I asked myself, trying to gain control.

We were silent for a while. She finished the color and began cutting my hair.

"Maybe he's gay or something," she said.

"The thought has crossed my mind. His imitation of a Spanish gay guy is so good it's freaky. He even calls him Marcel." I imitated the way he says it with a lisp. We both laughed. "That would actually be an easier explanation than blaming myself."

My mind reeled as I considered the implications of all of this.

But where did that leave me? Stuck living with a non-sexual man for the rest of my life?

I had always thought I was being punished for my wild days in New York or for the married men I had dated. Of course, they had lied, but I thought somehow karma was getting back at me.

But, if it wasn't me, then what?

"So, what can I do? Live a life where I never have sex again? I'm only 50. Is this it for me?" I said out loud.

"Hmmm," she murmured as she evened out my bangs. "Let me think." She cut a little more off the sides.

"You need a boyfriend."

"Really?" I said, spitting out my wine. OK, I did have a crush on someone, but it was harmless and only existed in my mind. Physical cheating was something very different—once you crossed the line, there was no going back. It was like when I lost my virginity. I waited until college unlike most people I knew. But once I had done it once, it made it way easier to do it the next time.

If the problem wasn't me, then why should I live a life without sex? I pondered.

The lateness of the night stopped bothering me as my mind started thinking of the possibilities.

4 He's Back

Tom had been missing from the gym for a week. I was in a panic. He had never missed even one day before. I did my weights, trying to accept that he had changed gyms and I would never see him again.

I must have scared him away. My crush must have been way too obvious.

My heart felt like it was beating out of my chest.

Why was I so crazy? I wondered.

Because catching glimpses of him was so exciting. It was like a drug. The feeling motivated me to come even earlier each day.

What if he was really gone? What would I do?

I took a deep breath.

I won't die. I will survive this if he's gone. I will just find something else to feel good about. I will not die, I kept telling myself, hoping that maybe there was some kind of explanation for his absence.

I grabbed the back-machine handles, ready to pull them down.

Wait, was that Tom's reflection in the mirror behind me?

I squinted at the image.

Yes, it was.

I said a silent Hallelujah. I breathed deeply and tried to hide my smile. I hurriedly finished what I was doing and walked over to him.

"Where have you been?" I asked trying to sound nonchalant.

"I was fishing up north for a week with some friends," he said.

Phew, he didn't find a new gym.

I took a deep breath and grabbed hold of the wall near the machine to steady myself. I tried to imagine him waiting for the fish.

"What did you do all day? Was it boring or fun?"

"It was relaxing. I had a lot of time to sit and wait for fish—nothing to do but think," he said.

He was back. My whole body was relieved, and my muscles relaxed. I stared at his adorable smile. I automatically assumed that he was thinking about me. I was so relieved to see him that I didn't hear his question. He repeated it.

"What have you been up to?"

My punchiness caused my mouth to go on autopilot. "Well, I was getting my hair cut until 2:00 in the morning last night. I am so tired, and I just can't stop thinking about the conversation I had with Desiree, my hairdresser."

He took the bait. "What was it about?" he asked. I had moved with him to another nautilus machine. I no longer cared about my workout, so happy to be talking to him after the long, tortuous week.

"Basically, I was telling her that my husband is more like a room-mate or brother. We share a house but have no real connection—physically or emotionally."

"It sounds like you need a boyfriend," he said without hesitation.

Did he just say that?

I rubbed my ears, trying to clear them. I opened my mouth and stared. "What did you say?"

"You need to get a boyfriend," he repeated.

I closed one eye and squinted at him with the other. "I can't believe you said that. That's what Desiree said last night. Wow!"

I walked away with a smile on my face. He must want to be my boyfriend. Why else would he have said it? I was so happy I thought I would die. I walked around in a daze for the rest of the morning. My imagination ran wild. The dopamine from my thoughts was a happy drug. It helped fuel my fantasy. He became my new Paul McCartney. He wanted me. I began to create a whole life for us together in my mind.

Spouses became irrelevant. True love conquers reality. I mean, wouldn't Jack recognize that Tom and I were soul mates? He would never get in the way of that. I left the gym that day convincing myself, as crazy as it sounds now, that our destiny was to be together.

5 Why was I Acting so Goofy?

Okay, so it sounded like a romance novel, but of course I love those books. They were the perfect fantasy. The girl and the guy were destined to be together, no matter the odds. They lived happily ever after in the end. Making this up in my mind just made me happy. It wasn't hurting anybody. It replaced the need to eat to numb my pain, and it didn't have calories.

I recently read a book that went through the science of this "happy effect." The basis of buzz appears to be a high degree of activity in a network of structures in the brain—often called the reward system. There is a neurotransmitter—a chemical that carries information between brain cells—called dopamine. It is the "reward chemical" released in response to anticipated pleasures. Cocaine and heroin, which stimulate dopamine-releasing neurons in humans, make people euphoric, confirming what some doctors have suggested.

I was literally feeling drugged. I became addicted to this feeling of pleasure. It felt real, even though it was only in my mind. I never thought I would be looking at other men, but if this is what it took to feel happy again, I didn't care. After years of feeling miserable, I didn't want to go back. I was hooked on feeling good.

I did a research project on marriage in college, and the results shocked me. I had to present an oral report to my sociology class, and I was so upset by my findings that it took me weeks to have the courage to present them. Seventy-five percent of those interviewed had been unfaithful in their marriages. I was distraught. Was I naïve? I asked my professor when I finally presented my report. "Could this be true?" I thought all people were faithful. I didn't get it.

My professor was great. He said that maybe it wasn't clear which people had participated in the study. We didn't know what audience was surveyed, and we could question the accuracy due to the sample population.

I felt a little better about it but still felt surprised. I assumed that when you were married, you were faithful. I started questioning married life in general and why people didn't remain true like they did in my happy-ending books.

After experiencing the pleasure of my fantasy with Tom, I started to understand it. At home I felt unimportant and not heard. Jack was not interested in me. It was a terrible feeling. I hadn't been aware I had been numbing it for 16 years. It was hard to allow myself to feel the hurt, resentment, disappointment and hopelessness. In contrast, my new fantasy with Tom was something that felt great. While not real, it gave me hope and a future to live into that wasn't painful. I was not even considering letting it go and having to deal with reality at that time. As shameful as that may seem, I just wasn't.

6   More Gym Excitement

For the next few weeks, I began to search Tom out more and more, enjoying the drug-like happiness I experienced around him. I was addicted to the thrill.

I went to the gym every day, timing my workouts so I could be where he was. I couldn't leave if I knew he was still there. I stretched at the door waiting for him to walk out. I figured out what cars he drove and where he parked.

Some days we talked and some days we just waved to each other. I never considered that anything I was doing was wrong. I had a crush on someone other than my husband. Big deal. I never saw Tom outside of the gym and there was no physical contact at all, so how bad could it be? And the best part, it wasn't causing me to gain weight.

I knew I was obsessed and out of control, but the thought of missing an opportunity to see Tom caused me such anxiety that I didn't care. I was so happy in my mind that I didn't try to fight it.

In my secret moments, I imagined our life together. I was happy, believing we were soul mates and knowing that with him, there would be no problems. We would live until old age together, happy and content. The fact that we were both married to other people was not a problem. In all my happy-ending books, love triumphed over reality. That's just the way it went. There was no other option. I walked around with my little secret. It made tolerating my real life that much easier, even though it only existed in my head.

7 What do you Wear to the Gym? The Magic Pants!

Every time I got dressed to go to the gym, I thought of my conversation with my hairdresser, Desiree. We had talked about how I was branching out of my corner at the gym and had begun to meet people.

"What do you wear there?" she asked.

Embarrassed, I changed the subject to avoid answering, but the question nagged at me. I was still wearing my Costco black capri pants and a shorter more fitted t-shirt, but I certainly didn't look like the "Thin Moms."

I secretly started trying on fitted exercise pants whenever I saw them in a store. I tried on over a hundred pairs. I'd pull each one on hoping it might be "the one that looks good." But after seeing my overly emphasized thigh chunks breaking up the smooth black material of the pants, I would get depressed and walk out empty handed.

Each time, I vowed to give up the search until the next time I was sweating in my old capri pants. I'd propel myself to attack the stores again, repeating the cycle of hope, disgust and resignation. I never found a pair of pants that even came close to what I wanted.

On Thanksgiving weekend, we celebrated with my family at my sister's house in Pennsylvania. By Saturday, Haley and I were bored and wanted to get out of the house. I told her about my secret quest for new exercise clothes. Since she had a natural fashion sense and a great eye, I thought maybe she could help me. We decided to try looking at Dick's Sporting Goods.

I panicked when I saw the racks and racks of exercise pants. "I don't think I can do this to myself. How different can they be from the others I've already tried?" I muttered. "Let's get out of here."

But Haley had already started shopping. She needed some new clothes for gymnastics and was pulling through the shorts on the racks.

Sighing, I grabbed about 15 pairs in different styles and sizes. I took them into the dressing room with a silent hope that this time would be different. I pulled on the first pair and looked in the mirror. Immediately I ripped them off. I tried on the rest. Nothing. I went out and got another ten, and then another ten when those were all bad. I was about to rip the sixth pair off when my daughter said, "Wait."

"Why? I asked.

She looked me up and down. "Turn around."

"You're kidding, right?" I said.

"These could work." The pants were black lycra and fit me like a glove. They were compression pants and somehow compacted my thighs.

I stared at myself in the mirror. "Seriously?" I asked. I was afraid to think we might have found "the ones." "I don't know if I could wear these in public."

"I think you could, but let's take them back to Sherry's and ask her. She will be brutally honest." My sister, Sherry, was not known for holding back her opinion. I knew we'd be driving right by Dick's on the way home the next day, so I could return the pants then if I needed to.

We told Sherry we needed her opinion. I put on the pants and walked into the room holding my hands over my stomach. I was barely breathing. She looked me up and down and then told me to turn around.

"Yes," she said. "They look good."

"Are you sure? I feel naked."

"Yes," she said. "Go get a few pairs."

On the way home, we stopped by Dick's. I bought two more pairs of the Magic Pants, and a couple of shirts, as well!

8 Wearing the Magic Pants

Back at home Monday, I put on my new pants and looked in the mirror. I grabbed a pair of sweats and put them on over them. I got to the gym and went onto the elliptical.

No problem, I thought. *No one has to see me in these. I'm not ready for prime time.*

As I exercised, my legs started sweating and I became uncomfortable. After about ten minutes, I went into the locker room and took off the sweats.

I came back out and walked around the perimeter of the room with my back to the wall, trying to pretend that nothing was different. I slithered onto the same elliptical, trying to act normal.

Ernie was stretching right next to me. After a few minutes, he saw me and did a double take.

"Hey, what have you got on there?" He asked. He walked closer to see the back of me. "Nice butt. Where have you been hiding that? Wow."

"You don't think it's obscene?" I asked, feeling my face turn Valentine red.

"Nope. You look great. Nice job. I am really proud of you."

"Thanks, Ernie," I said. I pumped my legs a few more times, jumped off the elliptical and grabbed him in a bear hug. It was awkward since we weren't evened out. I adjusted the angles of the hug. The people around us were staring, but I didn't care.

I took a deep breath, reveling in the relief. I hadn't realized how nervous and self-conscious I had been. Tears came to my eyes as, again, I held on longer than I should, not wanting to let go.

I think I'm really doing it this time, I thought to myself. *He said, "Nice butt."*

I thought of the sticker on the fridge that my father had put up for my sisters and me: "Boys Don't Make Passes at Girls with Fat Asses." Each time I saw it, I felt a silent stab in my heart, a reminder that my butt was not desirable. Well, fuck you, sticker! Today had become "Nice Butt Appreciation Day" for me.

I kissed Ernie on the cheek. "Thanks. I needed some courage." I let him go and got back on the elliptical, smiling so hard that my cheeks hurt.

When I was done, feeling brave, I walked through the men's weight section to the stretching area. Ernie came over to me and whispered, "I was walking behind you and saw the guys watch you as you walked by."

"And?" I asked afraid of what he would say.

"They were definitely appreciating those new pants. I would say very much so," he said, nodding.

Maybe someone else would have been embarrassed or horrified to know this, or think it was sexist, but I was thrilled. I stretched over my right leg. Could I be the old Hilary again—fun, enjoying life, and loving that people were watching me?

I stretched over my left leg. I'd been so afraid that Weight Watchers would be like all the other times I tried to lose weight. I'd still be Fat Hilary, hiding in the corner. My shoulders relaxed. I took a deep breath. My head got higher. Tears came to my eyes as relief filled me again.

I walked by Tom, my crush, on my way out. I waved. I saw him do a double take. I resisted the urge to turn around. I walked to my car with a big smile on my face. When I got into my car, I screamed and pumped both fists in the air, "Hallelujah," I yelled.

9 The Athlete Returns

I couldn't find Tom one Saturday at the gym. I was missing my buzz. I needed to distract myself. I wandered around the gym wondering what I could do to feel better. I ran into Big and Tall Scott.

"What are you doing?" he asked. "You look lost."

"I guess I am," I said absently. I looked inside the glass exercise room where a bunch of women were starting to go in. I looked at the schedule. It wasn't a Zumba class. Scott pushed me towards the room.

I moved in closer to the window. Inside, the women were positioning their step boxes and water bottles. They all looked thin and fit, wearing tight exercise pants or shorts, with matching snug little tops in vibrant colors.

As I watched, I felt a tightness in my chest as I remembered what happened five years before. I had switched from the local YMCA to this gym and was excited that they offered the same classes I used to take in New York. I had gone into the exercise room enthusiastic and innocent, hoping that my baggy shorts and loose t-shirt would hide my extra pounds. I got overwhelmed when I couldn't figure out which equipment to use. There was a frenzy of people grabbing weights, steps, and bars and there were none left by the time I figured out what was going on. I just stood there feeling stupid, fat and out of place. After I grabbed what remnants I could find, I picked a spot and started putting my equipment down, hoping I had everything I needed.

"This spot is taken," a woman said, starting to kick my stuff away with her foot.

"But there's no one here," I answered.

"Well, my friend Anne always stands here. This is her place." She continued to kick my weights.

Too shocked to respond, I gathered up my stuff and left, barely able to put it away before I burst into tears.

If I wasn't overweight, I bet she would have welcomed me, I thought.

I ran out of the room. I hadn't gone back.

Instead, I stayed hidden all those years on my elliptical machine in the corner. I was safe there and my extra weight was hidden from regular gym traffic. I told myself that jumping around with this oversized body would be too painful. Fat Hilary was just fine right where she was. Every time I had the urge to try a class, the thought of public humiliation squashed it.

"Why is this different than Zumba?" Scott asked, interrupting my negative trip down memory lane. "You love that now."

"Good question." I looked into the room again. "Zumba has no equipment and no saved spots. This is way scarier. Look at those ladies. They have perfect bodies and are very intense."

"Just go do it," he said.

"Hmmmmm," I murmured. I HAD lost 20 pounds and felt way better than six years before when I was traumatized by "Anne's friend." I was even wearing my magic, sleek black compression pants. It wasn't Lulu Lemon, but it was closer than my oversized shorts. Plus, I wanted a new challenge.

Why shouldn't I try it? Were they any better than me?

I moved closer to the window, causing it to fog up. I wiped it off. I watched the women laughing and talking to each other, relaxed and at ease. They all had their spots. My body tensed knowing the class was starting in three minutes.

What should I do? I wondered. Breathe, I thought.

I took my hair tie and started putting my hair into a ponytail.

I took another breath and walked in, wondering if I was making the right decision.

"Are you new? I don't recognize you. Grab a step."

Surprised, I looked up.

Was she talking to me?

She was and was obviously a regular in the class. I went and got a step from the case she was pointing to.

"You can set up right in front of me. There is room here. I'm Susan," she said and put out her hand.

Well, that's a change already, I thought.

I shook her hand and introduced myself. The warm-up was fun, and I had no trouble doing the repetitive step ups and side steps.

This is easy. I don't know why I was making such a big deal about it.

But then they started the real routine. Out of nowhere, the ladies were spinning, sashaying, stepping and leaping, fast and furiously. They all knew what they were doing and moved in unison, knowing the names of each segment as the instructor called them out.

I stood there frozen, afraid that once again I would burst into tears. I grabbed my step, ready to leave.

"Hang in there," Susan whispered. "We were all new once. Don't give up. It can only get better."

I stayed, resisting the strong urge to run out. Susan kept encouraging me, especially when the class ended. I told her I would come back and each class got a little bit easier.

One day we were doing a particularly hard pattern. I kicked the step out of frustration, feeling like I would never get it. With each repetition, though, I was able to do a little bit more. All of a sudden, I was turning, kicking and stepping in unison with the rest of the women.

FINDING THE OLD HILARY AGAIN

And then, as I danced, I was hit by a realization, something important that I had completely forgotten. I used to be an athlete—swim team, cheerleading and tennis team in high school, and captain of the varsity squash team in college. I had taken hundreds of exercise classes when I lived in New York City, and not once was I afraid. How had I forgotten all this?

Where had that girl gone?

I was so lost in thought I missed a step. My pulse raced. I realized how close I had come to twisting my ankle. I stopped to compose myself and then proceeded to do the whole routine perfectly. My head and chested lifted, feeling proud that I had pushed myself way beyond what was comfortable. The euphoria I felt matched the thrill of talking to a cute guy you've had a crush on for a while.

I looked in the mirror. I was drenched in sweat and breathing hard trying to catch my breath. I grabbed my water bottle and realized that after all these weeks, not only was I dancing in unison with the rest of the women, but I felt like I belonged here. I was one of them and even had my own spot on the floor. I looked outside the glass window almost expecting to see Fat Hilary still looking in longingly, but she was gone. The athlete had returned.

10 How Could I have Forgotten who I was?

How could I forget I had been an athlete? Good question. How could I have forgotten I had a brain, was fun or was capable of anything? More good questions.

Like I had said, when Jack and I were dating, he was my biggest champion. When I walked down that aisle, I was happy and sure that we could talk about anything and resolve any issues in communication.

But all that changed after our honeymoon and I didn't know why.

After all this time it's started to make sense.

Jack had his own incident growing up. His father left when he was 4. He couldn't have what he wanted which was to have his father stay, but he could become unassailable in an argument. He learned to do whatever he had to do to win.

"What are we going to do if your client stops paying you? How are we going to pay the bills? Don't you care what happens?" I'd ask him.

"How could you use the word care? That word is a stupid word," he'd counter.

"Well, then use another word. What happens if we lose your retainer? How will we pay the bills?" I'd ask.

"How we always pay them. What a stupid question. What is the problem now? Why are you always upset? Jesus."

This was way worse than him not listening. He would twist my words around, attack what I said, and put me on the defensive in a condescending tone of voice. He made sure that I knew I had asked a stupid question instead of answering it.

Not only did we never get to resolve any issues, but after being spoken to this way for years, my confidence was replaced. First with confusion

Was Jack right? Did he know better?

FINDING THE OLD HILARY AGAIN

Then with defeat. The confidence I had when I was single was slowly worn away with each argument.

Life was all about Jack.

If I questioned something, I was belittled. "Don't you think other women would be happy to have a guy like me? I could be out womanizing. Instead I am focused on our son."

After a time, instead of feeling like a huge, powerful person, I began feeling, like I had when I was little, like there was something wrong with me. I forgot anything good I had done and became a caged mouse. If I came out and tried to assert myself, Jack would dominate me back into the cage. It was easier to stay in there than to keep fighting a losing battle. When I started losing weight and feeling my emotions again, I realized how damaging this had been to my sense of self.

When I was in step class and mastered a very difficult routine, I was thrilled. I was happy. I felt great. And it burnt off some of the fog that had covered up my prior accomplishments. I really had forgotten them. They had disappeared for me. Because everything in my marriage had been about Jack and his hockey, Jack and who he knew, Jack and what he wanted. The Hilary I knew disappeared.

That is why the gym became my great escape and why I couldn't miss a day. I was okay there. I mattered. I felt good. I overcame my fears, and, most of all, I got glimpses of the old me. I could hold my own and not worry about being argued back into my cage.

11 It's Better this Way

On Monday mornings, my boss started having early meetings 45 minutes away from my house. In order to get there on time, I had to leave the gym by 6:20 to get home and shower. That meant I needed to arrive at the gym by 5:00. It took a little while to get used to, but I was willing to wake up earlier in order to get in my work out.

I knew Tom's schedule. He walked in at exactly 6:10 every morning. On Mondays, I knew he started on the chest machine right by the door. I strategically placed myself right behind the machine to stretch, knowing I would overlap with him for only a few minutes.

For an hour and a half, I looked forward to my precious minutes with Tom. That morning, I watched him walk in, go into the locker room and come out. My heart was beating fast.

He sat at the chest machine like he did every Monday.

"Hey," I said from around the back.

"Go away," Tom said.

I thought he was kidding. "How are you?" I asked.

"I said go away. I'm not in the mood."

I was stunned. This was not what I expected. I felt like I had been slapped. Just as I had learned when I was little, I pretended I was fine and didn't say a word. I grabbed my stuff and hurried out of the gym.

What did I do wrong? Why did he act like that?

BEEP! I swerved and barely missed a car coming into the gym parking lot.

I drove home, arms still tingling from my near accident.

Thank you, God, for saving me again. I need to wake up and pay attention. But why was Tom so mean?

I turned right, swinging extra wide and barely missed another car.

What was wrong with me?

I felt like crying.

I lived for those few minutes with Tom. I guess it wasn't the same for him. The thought was too upsetting to dwell on.

Get a grip, I told myself, grimacing from the exhaust from the school bus in front of me.

I've made up this whole thing, and he's obviously an asshole and not who I thought he was. And he just has no fucking interest. It's time for me to get real.

It's better this way. I'll just focus on my marriage like I should have been doing all along. It's time to see if I can make things work with Jack. Maybe my crush on Tom is the reason that things aren't working at home.

12 Phoenix

It was perfect timing for my new marriage resolution. I had won a long-weekend AFLAC trip to a five-star resort in Phoenix. Jack and I were leaving the next day. I had been worried that I'd be wishing I was with Tom instead of Jack, but now that would not be an issue. I could focus on Jack and make sure we had a wonderfully romantic five days. Again, Jack's lack of romance never entered my mind. I quickly replaced Tom with Jack in my unrealistic fantasy.

Since I was a little girl, I had always wanted a romantic, loving marriage. Buried very deep in my brain, despite any notions of my real life, I hung onto the thought that I could still somehow have one. It kept the hope alive that somehow Jack and I could work things out.

Did I ask Jack for what I wanted? Of course not. In my fantasy life the man knows what I want. He's my knight in shining armor. There is no reason to speak up. I am the princess. I just silently expected things to be the way I wanted. It makes no sense now, but back then it's just the way it was.

We had an early flight the next morning to Arizona. At the hotel, we worked out in the little gym and then floated luxuriously in a narrow circular pool. The man-made current took us slowly around the grounds on our rafts. For the first time in many years, I felt relaxed, happy to be away from the stresses of everyday living. The few white puffy clouds turned into one dark angry one. I put on my long-sleeved shirt, shivering, and we went up to the room.

There were two beds in the room.

What am I supposed to do? I wondered.

Jack and I hadn't been alone together much at all since we had had kids. I felt embarrassingly shy. Nervously, I grabbed my book and started reading.

I felt Jack's eyes on me. "You want to fool around?" he asked.

Shocked, I looked at him.

Not really, I thought, *but if I say no, there may never be another chance.*

"Okay," I said.

We undressed quickly. But by the time I was aroused, Jack was done. Before I could say "What about me?" he had put on one of the fluffy white hotel bathrobes and headed out to our little deck to read the paper. I just lay on the bed, too stunned to speak.

I closed my eyes, feeling dirty. I could understand feeling used after a one-night stand, but this was my husband. He was supposed to care about me. The rough bedspread was scratchy, and the taste left from his sour breath disgusted me.

I got under the soft, clean sheets. After dozing off for a while I got up to take a shower. I stood under the water and remembered feeling the same after an incident when Jack and I were engaged…

I had decided to surprise Jack, who had made fun of my cotton underpants, by spending an afternoon shopping at Victoria's Secret. According to my friend Betsy who was helping me, her boyfriend went crazy when she wore this stuff. They had wild sex all night every time. I smiled as I anticipated Jack ripping it off me in a fit of passion.

That night, I came out of the bathroom in one of my new bra and panty sets, shyly, but with anticipation.

Jack took one look at me and turned back towards the TV, pointing the remote control and changing the channel. He never looked back. I couldn't move or speak. After a few painful minutes, I turned around and went into the bathroom. I put on my old stuff and sat on to the toilet for a while. I couldn't think of what I could possibly say. Betsy had practically promised that we would have great sex. What had gone wrong? When I finally came out, unable to speak up, I pretended that nothing had happened.

It took me two months to bring it up. We were walking on the streets of Paris, having gone over for New Year's Eve to celebrate our engagement. We were walking by a lingerie store and I snapped. The resentment and hurt had built up and burst out of my mouth before I could stop it.

"Why didn't you do something when I had that Victoria's Secret underwear on?" I screamed, shoving him as hard as I could against the side of the lingerie store.

"I don't know," he said, not looking me in the eyes. After a few minutes he added, "I guess I didn't like what you bought."

"Are you kidding me?" I cried. "Do you know what it took for me to spend five hours at Victoria's Secret torturing myself? I hated every minute of it, but I did it for you. Betsy said that we would have great sex if I did it. And all you did was change the channel." I was sobbing at this point.

Jack looked at me like a little boy who didn't know what he had done to make his mother mad. He thought about it for a few minutes.

"Well, why don't we go together, and I'll help you pick out what I like," he said quietly.

Temporarily mollified, I agreed. We went to Victoria's Secret together when we got back home, and I let him dress me. He preferred thongs with matching bras that had no support. I hated the permanent wedgy and feeling like my boobs were falling out, so I only wore "his picks" when he would see them. But in the end, it made no difference.

Our sex life did not improve.

Still standing under the water in the shower, I felt numb.

Every book I had ever read said that a man's biggest problem was not getting enough sex. How did I get the one guy on earth who barely wanted any?

And, now that I had had it, I felt worse than before. I needed to get out of there.

I quietly got dressed and went down to the bar. I found my friends from AFLAC and proceeded to drink and eat for the rest of the trip—bacon cheeseburgers, curly fries, beer and nachos and margaritas. And to make it worse, the weather stayed cloudy, cold, and gloomy, unusual for the desert.

13 Is It Me?

We got home from our trip. I went to the gym and Tom was there. He apologized for his bad mood that day.

"My uncle died," he said. "I didn't sleep much. I'm sorry I took it out on you."

It was enough to restart my fantasy. In it, I was unconditionally loved by Tom. After Phoenix, I had once again given up on ever having the kind of physical relationship I wanted with Jack.

Disappointing as that was, our financial situation was even more stressful. Jack and I had very different philosophies about money. He loved to spend and have debt, and I loved to save. In order to try to salvage the situation, I made myself responsible for our finances.

Shortly after Phoenix, I sat down at the computer since it was time to pay the bills.

I can handle this, I told myself.

I took out the stack of envelopes. I was not going to let this get to me this time.

I removed the bills from the envelopes, sorted them by due date, and calculated what we owed. I went online to look at our account balances.

Not good, I thought.

Sitting at the computer, facing the wall, I figured out which bills we could pay.

If we covered the mortgage and the car payments, we couldn't pay the local taxes, life insurance, home equity loan, cable, electric or water. How had this happened, I often asked myself, even though I knew the story.

Jack had stopped practicing law when his one client stopped paying his retainer. He told Jack not to come back unless they asked him to. It was disturbing since we were then solely relying on our AFLAC commissions to pay our bills. We were new and hadn't developed any renewal income yet. We only made money when we made sales. It was unpredictable and unreliable.

I looked at Jack, sprawled on the couch watching hockey. He had a drink in his hand.

It doesn't look like he's upset about this. I think I'll join him.

I went into the kitchen, opened a bottle of wine, and poured myself a hefty glass. Then I grabbed the chips and hummus for moral support. I walked back to the computer.

"Jack," I said, trying to keep my voice neutral. "Is there any more money coming in this month? I can barely pay a third of our bills."

"Don't worry," Jack said, like he always did, and changed the channel between hockey games.

"But I am worried. Each month I think it's going to be better, and it's getting worse instead."

"I'll take care of it." He slurped loudly on his vodka and tonic.

I hate that sound, I thought.

"What's the problem?" he asked, taking another loud slurp.

I grimaced and said, "It stresses me out,"

... along with that noise you are making.

"I'm trying to get ahead of the bills so I can pay for Haley's cheerleading. I'm really frustrated." I pulled the mascara off my eyelashes, a nervous habit I had developed. I looked at the eyelash on my finger. Shit. If these don't grow back, I will be eyelash-less.

"I think we're doing fine," Jack said. "Don't I always get the bills paid?"

"I don't call it getting them paid when you have to borrow money from the equity in our home. Our debt is growing, and our income is not. I hate living like this."

"What do you want me to do? Yell? Cry? Scream? Would that make you feel better?" He started walking around screaming and waving his arms like a two-year-old having a tantrum. "Is this what you want?"

He started jumping up and down pulling at his hair. "Does this make you feel better?"

"No," I said. "Please stop that."

"You're never happy with the amount of money I make, are you? A lot of women would be happy to have a guy like me."

"No, I never said that. It's how you manage money that bothers me."

"What? Do you want to sell the house? We could pay it all off and put it under our mattress. Is that what you want?"

"No, I just want you to understand what I'm saying so we can have a different life," I said quietly. I gave up and just walked away. It beat continuing to get beat up with his words and sarcasm.

I went outside, wondering how I had married someone who had such a different way of handling money. I should have known. When Jack and I returned from our engagement trip to Paris, we got bored on the plane ride home and started looking at the duty-free items. Jack encouraged me to buy $150 Hermes scarves for our mothers. My instincts were screaming no. I was eager to please him, though, so I went along with it. His mother loved her scarf, but my mother was upset that I had spent so much.

The next lightbulb went off a few months after we got married. I had left my job in New York to start my own personal coaching business. The first few months were okay, but by the time I was pregnant, my income could barely cover the cost of the apartment I had in New York. I had owned it when I lived in the city and had not yet been able to sell it. I rented it out when I could, but it wasn't really allowed since it was a co-op.

I finally sold it later that year for a loss.

My coaching income had dwindled, and, for the first time since college graduation, I didn't have my own spending money. When I became pregnant, I asked Jack if it was okay if I bought some maternity clothes.

"Sure," he said. "Buy whatever you need."

Really? I thought. *Buy whatever I need?"*

It was a new experience for me. I bought a few outfits that my growing body could fit into and look halfway decent. It was nice being able to treat myself to new clothes. When I was single, I was very strict with my money and rarely bought entire outfits. A pair of pants or shoes on sale, maybe, but never an entire outfit. This was fun.

I wasn't used to it. Growing up, we were told that my grandmother bought bruised fruit to save money. And I remember getting a touch tone phone in college that cost 25 cents more per month. My parents couldn't believe how extravagant I was. I decided that "wasting" money was wrong and something to be criticized for.

When I was single, I put my raises into savings and continued to live on a lower standard of living. At some level, I felt noble about it. I felt extravagant when I bought clothes or took vacations, even though I had the money saved. Having a balance on a credit card was beyond the scope of my thinking. Why would someone purposely create debt and interest expense? I couldn't even think about it.

And, like with sex, I just thought that when we got married, everything would be good. Jack would think like me and everything would be fine. In my mind, Jack had enough money to pay for these clothes or he wouldn't have said to buy them. I didn't think twice about it.

I couldn't understand why Jack kept complaining that there was no money left after he paid the bills each month.

That's impossible, I thought. *His one client was paying him $20,000 per month. That was way more than I ever made and must be way more than we needed. Wasn't it? How could there be nothing left?*

I made an appointment with his secretary and we went over all the bills. Jack would pay the bills, but she would enter them in QuickBooks, so she had access to them. We calculated the total and his income covered it. What was the problem? I asked.

She took out three envelopes and handed them to me with a wicked grin as if to say, "You married him, not me." There were three different credit cards. I looked at this month's charges. There were meals, office expenses, clothes he had bought, gas and other expenses.

I totaled the outstanding balances. It was over $10,000. I felt sick seeing my new clothes on one of the bills.

"How did the balances get so high?" I asked. "Doesn't he pay them off each month?"

"No, he pays what he can. He never has enough to pay them off. And, over time, the balances just keep getting higher. He doesn't worry about it. He's always done it this way."

Sixteen years later he still did. It didn't bother him, but it bothered me. The thought made me sick.

I was not raised to have debt. I was raised to save. But instead, all I could do was damage control. And I wasn't doing a very good job.

On my way to the gym every day I would check our balances. If Jack was negative, I tried to cover it before the bank charged us. If I was too late, I beat myself up for wasting money on needless bank fees. I used whatever money I had put aside to cover his spending. There was never any money left to do other things. I hated always saying no to the kids.

I felt like I was drowning. Instead of turning the Titanic in a different direction, I was sinking with it with no way to stop it.

I tried to talk to Jack. I developed budgets. I tried to get him off the credit cards. But he didn't understand what I was saying, and nothing ever changed. He just ended every conversation by saying I was just crazy. There was nothing to be upset about. He had it under control.

The next day at the gym I again wondered if Jack was right. Was it me? Was I just negative? Was I just looking for something to be upset about? Was there even a problem? I could see my arms shaking as I pushed the levers harder on the elliptical. I felt like my head was going to explode. Maybe I really was going crazy.

I saw Ernie, my high school friend, coming toward the weight area to my right.

Thank God, I thought.

I jumped off the machine and ran over to him. I grabbed him and looked at him straight in the eyes.

"Ernie, tell me the truth. Is it me? Am I just crazy?" My tears broke loose. I didn't care if people saw me crying. I needed to know. I told him what happened.

"Hilary, I've told you before, it's not you. You are fine. You need to get out of there. He is not good for you. He is manipulating your mind."

"He is?" I asked, wiping my eyes with the back of my hand.

"Yes, look at yourself. You were never like this before. Did you have money problems when you were single?"

"No," I said.

"Did you have a good life and get to do what you wanted financially?"

"Yes."

"Can you do that now?"

"No," I said and burst into tears again. I was crying so hard my shoulders were shaking. I kept my head down so that the people staring could not meet my eyes. I knew I was making a scene, but it felt good to release the pressure and frustration from years of financial stress.

"Hang in there," Ernie said.

I walked away, keeping my head down. I looked around for something to wipe my nose with. Making even more of a scene, I ran the 30 feet into the locker room holding my nose and grabbed some tissues. I wasn't ready to go home.

I went into the corner to stretch, facing the wall so no one could see me.

Was Jack really manipulating me?

I hadn't thought about that before. Maybe that wasn't the right word.

Maybe dismissing me or ignoring me was better, I thought, stretching over my right leg.

I mean, I have a business degree from Wharton, for God's sake, which I keep forgetting for some reason. Ernie's right. I saved money when I was single and always had money for vacations, savings, fun, whatever I wanted. I enjoyed my life. There was no concern about money. So how did I let this happen? I hated my life now. The best it ever got was to be able to pay another bill. I was making money to pay for what Jack had already spent. I never did anything because I didn't feel right spending money we didn't have.

I blew my nose. I had let Jack shut me up over and over by telling me I was crazy. I kept trying to make budgets or eliminate the credit cards or do whatever I could do to turn around our finances. Jack would listen, agree, make promises and act like he was on board with my plan.

These conversations usually happened on Sundays. I would get excited to finally make more, save more and reduce our debt. I would start thinking about the kind of life I had when I was single. Savings in the bank, taking vacations, buying things with cash and having no credit card debt.

I believed him every time. I got my hopes up. I thought it could work. But by Tuesday or Wednesday when Jack was still doing the same things, running up negative balances and using credit cards, I would get suspicious.

"Jack, you said you were going to stick to the budget and check with me if you were going to buy something that wasn't planned for," I'd say. "Why did you just go spend $300 at Costco? We didn't need all this food. It's just going to go bad. You said you were going to check with me first. I don't get it."

"I would never say that. Those are not the words I would ever say," Jack said.

"I heard you. I swear. You agreed. Why didn't you follow the plan?"

"I would never have agreed to that. I think you just like to be upset. What's the problem? I don't see a problem. I'll pay it off. I always do. What is wrong with you?"

The cycle continued. I really didn't know how to make him stick to my plan. In the end, my negative driveway pattern would take over and cover over my disappointment.

It's my fault. I'm stupid for having gotten my hopes up. What an idiot I am. I can't have what I want. I knew it was too good to be true.

And I would give up.

Eventually I would stop being a victim and start the endless cycle of planning, promises, excitement and disappointment again.

But nothing was different. Jack never changed his actions.

Over time, the little bits of overspending added up to a lot of debt. I hated not being able to turn around the sinking ship.

I got up to find Ernie. "I think you're right. He makes promises and doesn't keep them. Then he acts like I'm the problem. But what can I do? I feel like I'm stuck in a bad dream here."

"Hilary, you've made a lot of progress in the past couple of years. Look how great you look. You just need to get away from him."

I thought about it for a little while. "But what if I end up alone?"

"Are you kidding? Lots of guys here are already interested in you. They think you are hot."

"Me? Seriously?" I said with my mouth open.

"Yes. A bunch of them. Look, I have to go. See you tomorrow."

I grabbed him for a quick hug. "Thanks, Ernie," I said. "You don't know how much I needed to hear this today. I really felt like I was going insane."

"I know," he said. "But you're doing great. You can do this."

I watched him leave. I had a lot to think about. But even so, I was distracted wondering who said I was hot. I hoped it was Tom. How could I find out?

Please, please let him be one of them.

I started smiling as I walked out to my car.

14 Background on Finances

I still wonder how two people with Ivy League educations had gotten into this financial situation. Jack had a law degree and had practiced law for 30 years. I had a business degree, had been a management consultant, and worked on Wall Street. It still baffles me to this day.

When we first got married, Jack had one main legal client. Ninety percent of his income came from this childhood friend's business. I remember being concerned that he was so dependent on the good will of this friend.

What if they sold the business? What if they got a new lawyer? What would we do?

Jack made good money, but he never searched out new business and didn't diversify his income.

After we got married, my own coaching business was very different from the salaried life in the corporate world. Running a business on my own for the first time, I made many mistakes that cost me money.

If someone didn't show up for an appointment, I found it hard to reach them to set the next one. When someone stuck with it and hit their goals, I didn't think to sign them up for three more months, so they stopped coaching with me. When my initial clients finished, I didn't fully replace them with new ones.

I had already gone through my warm leads when I moved to Connecticut after our wedding. It was hard to find new clients. When I had my first child, I was consumed with the baby and the business died a natural death. Jack's income, once sufficient, became a growing concern a few years later when his one client started reducing what they paid him.

We began to look at home-based businesses I could work at while being there for the kids, and we found one. I loved the part of the job where I would meet people and be out with adults at night. We achieved a certain level of success, and I achieved my dream of speaking to groups all over the country.

The problem was that we never replaced Jack's legal income. Over time, we tried about 12 other businesses, investing thousands of dollars in the process. We ended up spending money instead of making money.

One day at the gym, I was on the elliptical wondering what had happened to my confidence. When I was single in the city, you couldn't mess with me. I got a job right out of college, and my income had grown significantly over the years. I was recruited away from my first consulting job and placed on Wall Street. I took jobs for granted since it hadn't been an issue to get one back then.

When the kids got big enough to go to school, I redid my resume and sent it to a headhunter. I followed up a few days later, confident that she would be impressed with my background, and eager to start working.

"Honey," she said sounding like Mae West, "I'm having trouble placing people who've been out of the work force for six months, let alone 14 years. I'm not going to be able to help you."

I was stunned. I had never considered this. What the heck had happened? I put down the phone. Another dash to my confidence. I remember feeling embarrassed. I think that's when I lost a little more of my groove.

When we found AFLAC, our 12th business, money came into our bank account instead of going out.

Finally, I thought.

I started working full time at AFLAC. I didn't have much confidence as a salesperson, but the people were fun. I never thought I would be selling insurance, but since money was coming in, I was encouraged.

Commission sales meant we only made money if we made a sale. It made it difficult at the beginning. What saved us was Jack's remaining law income. His monthly retainer paid the mortgage. We could use the AFLAC money to pay the rest.

Then his client stopped paying the retainer. I got scared. Some months our AFLAC money was ok, but sometimes it wasn't. Jack didn't mind using the checking-plus lines to fill in the gaps. I hated it. It made me feel like I was sinking into an abyss.

Jack didn't care. No matter what I said, it didn't matter.

When the credit balances at the bank got really high, Jack would happily use the home equity line of credit to pay them down to zero. He seemed to think the credit line was free money, there to be used. The balance on the home equity line grew over time to the point I was afraid we would have no equity left in the house. Jack also kept refinancing the regular mortgage. Instead of paying it down over the years, we owed almost double what we had paid for the house.

None of this bothered Jack. He was used to having a sporadic cash flow in the legal business, but I was not. I hated not knowing how we would pay the bills. I was not very confident and struggling in sales. I was good at the back end but wary of approaching companies and following up. I knew I wasn't contributing enough but felt confused about what to do about it. I was dependent on Jack to make the sales, and his confidence and success went in cycles.

Sales wasn't my thing. I started slowly, using accounting firms and consulting firms as my first clients since I was familiar with them. Then I had an encounter of the worst kind with my first manager at AFLAC. We were standing in an underground parking garage after meeting with a client. He was hung over and yelling at me.

"Why were you arguing with me in there? Why were you interrupting me when I was talking? Why were you talking to the woman next to you?" he said.

"I thought my job was to schmooze the client. She was asking me questions," I replied.

"But I was trying to do my presentation. You interrupted the flow."

"I'm sorry, I didn't know. I thought I was doing what I was supposed to do."

"No. I can't believe you did that. You lost us the client."

He kept going on for 45 minutes. I started crying and apologizing and begged him to stop, but he wouldn't. He just kept going with his tirade. I was afraid to just walk away since he was my boss. I was dependent on him as a new agent. Part of our income was from him bringing us into his client accounts to help. I tried to tell him that I thought I was doing what I was supposed to do.

"No!" he said nastily. "You were arguing with me. You ruined everything."

After that day, my old pattern of not trusting my instincts kicked in. For six months, I got quiet and stayed in the background, letting Jack go out and get the clients. I worked on the admin and told myself I was horrible at sales. I didn't even try to look for new clients. The longer I went without doing it, the less and less faith I had in myself, which is deadly in the sales profession.

"I just have to change my thinking," I thought, pushing the elliptical harder. "And stop being a scared victim." Right out of college I was fearless, confident and secure in my ability to support myself. I hated that now I was dependent on Jack and the moods of mean bosses.

"It's enough," I said, taking my frustration out on my elliptical. "Action conquers fear. I want to become a woman who can support herself with confidence again."

15 Steve's Button

"What's this?" I asked. I had been walking by the men's locker room at the gym and someone handed me a business card.

"My band is playing next month. Why don't you come?"

"I'd love to. What kind of music?"

"Everything."

"Sounds fun. Are you Steve?" I asked, reading the card a little closer.

"Yes. That's me."

"Nice to meet you after all this time. I'm Hilary."

I had been watching Steve for a while. He was a little unusual, to say the least. He had dark skin and crazy hair, and he always wore a white muscle shirt under a loose hoodie. He wore gold chains and blue and white lean fitting sweatpants. And, most noticeably, he was loud. From my perch on my favorite elliptical in the little alcove, I could always hear Steve coming. I used to watch him and wonder what was up with this guy. This was the first time we had talked.

"Hey, Hilary, that green looks great on you," he yelled loudly across the weight area the next day.

"My, don't you look nice in red," he yelled the day after that. "And your hair looks good, too."

After several days of this, I couldn't take it anymore. "Steve, I'd love it if these compliments were real, but I think you just say this kind of stuff to everyone."

"You don't believe me?" His brown compassionate eyes looked straight into mine.

"I want to, but since I'm not really used to people saying nice things, I'm figuring you just say this to everyone and don't really mean it," I said, my voice breaking.

"Well, I wouldn't say it if I didn't believe it. You really do look great every day. I don't know how your hair looks that good at 5:00 AM. Most people are wearing baseball caps if you've noticed."

I looked around at the other females. He was right.

"I guess I do have good hair. You're not just floating my boat with all the nice compliments?"

"I'm really not."

My eyes started welling up. I took a deep breath, reveling in the new feeling of being admired.

"I actually really love when you say these things. It seems like all I am is put down at home. I don't hear many positive things about myself. Can I take a little mini Steve home

FINDING THE OLD HILARY AGAIN

with me? I'll just put him on my bathroom counter, and he can tell me how good I look every day."

"Sure," he said.

A few days later, I saw Steve as I was walking in. "My, don't you look good in blue," he yelled across the floor.

We both smiled knowingly. "This is great. What if I press your button when I need a compliment?" I pressed my index finger against his chest.

"Gee, your cheeks look nice and round," he said with a mischievous smile.

I giggled. I pressed "the button" again.

"My, your eyes look blue today." We both laughed so hard we had to bend over. He grabbed the rope and started doing triceps.

"You have to squeeze this," he said, handing me the bottom of the rope.

"Like this?" and I gestured suggestively. Again, we were laughing so hard we couldn't stop.

"It feels so good to laugh," I said. "A little Steve in the morning and life is good."

As I worked out, I thought about it—compliments, a positive uplifting friend, and laughter. What a different feeling from how I felt walking in after my fight with Jack that morning.

I was in the bathroom, putting on my make-up, trying not to wake him up since it was 4:30 AM.

"How come you look so nice when you go to the gym?"

I jumped. Jack came out of the dark hall into the light of the bathroom. His sarcasm dripped nastiness all over my good mood.

"It makes me feel better about myself," I said, keeping my head down.

"Well, how come you don't make the effort when you are at home with me?" he asked.

Because you don't notice me or care, I thought.

"Good question," I said.

I finished applying my mascara and dug for my lipstick in my cosmetic bag.

I tried for years, and you never noticed, I thought. *Now, you want to know? Fuck you.*

But I didn't say anything. I knew I was no match for his ability to argue and I would lose.

"Don't engage," my friend, Renee had advised me. I didn't. If I started an argument, it would go on forever. My day would be ruined.

"Well, I resent the effort you make to look good for the guys at the gym," he said.

"I appreciate your communicating. Got to go," I said. I grabbed my bag and ran down the stairs.

As soon as I got in the car, the phone was ringing.

"Yes," I snarled.

"Why do the guys at the gym get more effort than I do? I don't get it," Jack said.

"I guess because they notice me and say nice things. It makes it worth the effort. I am not ignored there. And, they are nice."

"Well, it's easy for them to be nice. That's not real life. And, maybe I wouldn't ignore you if you tried to look a little better for me," he said.

"That's exactly why I don't," I said.

I slammed down the phone. I just want to be loved exactly as I am. I don't want to have to dress a certain way at home, for God's sake, to get a little attention. The only time Jack pays attention is when I'm trying to get out of the house. Otherwise, he doesn't seem to notice me.

My tears were coming down now. I did my abs in the corner of the gym.

Was Jack right? Had I let myself go at home? Was he justified in ignoring me? Does a wife need to always fix herself up to keep her man interested? Was it my fault?

Don't play that game, I told myself.

I wasn't heavy when we got married. I looked good, and Jack still didn't pay attention to me. He was busy leading seminars, then with hockey, on the computer or watching tv.

I asked him to pay attention to me, knowing it was my love language. And he couldn't be bothered. It wasn't his thing.

So why now did he notice me when I was getting ready to go to the gym? And why was he even up at 4:30 AM? Why couldn't he just ignore me now and make life less stressful? Was it only because I'm not letting him dominate me? Or because I'm happy again?

The truth was that I couldn't let myself care about what Jack thought or did. I was tired of feeling bad. I needed to focus on being positive. I wanted to feel better about myself instead of worse.

Steve's comments lifted me up. The heavy jacket of misery that I had put on to protect myself felt a little lighter. Having Steve recognize positive qualities in me made me feel good instead of bad. Laughing with Steve felt like drinking a healthy tonic. I needed to find more of this.

I looked around the gym and saw him at the leg press.

"Hey Steve," I yelled loudly. Some of the weightlifters looked at me startled.

I pressed Steve's chest. "Your smile lights up my day," he said, smiling widely.

"Thanks, Steve," I said giving him a one arm hug. "You are just what I needed today. Thanks." I gave him a peck on the cheek and ran out to my car.

16 Thin Mom, Me?

One day I had gone shopping for new clothes since my old ones were too big. A really nice problem to have. I was trying on my jeans and my daughter's mouth dropped open.

"Mom," she shouted. "Mom! You are wearing thin mom jeans. You are a thin mom."

"Really?" I said. Not really listening.

"Mom, you are not wearing Fat Mom Jeans right now. You are a Thin Mom."

My eyes welled up with tears. I thought about all those days on the playground watching the "thin moms" in their nice little skinny white jeans. I remember feeling bad about myself and thinking that I used to be like them in my younger days.

"Seriously?" I asked. "You're not kidding, right?"

"No, Mom. You really look good. You are a thin mom."

This may not seem like a big deal, but this was the little girl who told me I was old and wasn't supposed to look good. It made me feel proud and at the same time quite warm and fuzzy. I wasn't feeling invisible anymore. This was a big deal.

PART 4
———

Trouble

1   Who Said It?

One day at the gym, I was frustrated again after a night trying to pay our bills. I tried an elliptical in a different area of the gym.

Who are those two very fit, good-looking guys, I wondered? *I've never seen them on the other side of the gym. And look at that.*

I couldn't take my eyes off the very nice butt of the guy stretching in the area to my right.

I like it over here, I thought. *Better than watching TV.*

I momentarily forgot my money and relationship problems. Just then Ernie walked right in front of me.

"Hey Ernie," I yelled, jumping off my elliptical and running after him.

"Hey," he said, stopping and turning towards me. "What's going on?"

"Well, some weird guy was looking at me the other day, and remember you said some guys thought I was hot? Well, I was wondering if he was one of them…ummm…who exactly were they?" I was sort of mumbling, and it wasn't exactly true, but I couldn't think of anything else to say to figure out who had said I was hot.

He paused a moment before reaching for his arm machine. "Oh, let me think…Claudio, Joe, and of course Tom," he said.

Halle-freaking-lujah, I screamed inside my head.

In my mind, I was twirling around doing back handsprings. Outwardly, I said, "Oh, ok, thanks. I was just wondering. No biggie."

I walked off in a daze. *Yes, biggie. Tom thinks I'm hot. I wasn't imagining it.*

2 Is It in my Head?

In the next few weeks, my feelings spiraled even more out of control. I figured out what cars Tom drove, where he parked, and started tracking his moves at the gym. One day, walking on the treadmill, I watched him walk by. He didn't even look at me.

That is not how a man in love should be acting, I thought. I felt a dull ache in my stomach. *Could this all be in my mind? I mean, he's never asked for my number or wanted to see me outside of the gym. Am I just crazy?*

I felt a familiar ache in my back and stomach. I slowed down the treadmill, trying to figure out what was going on.

I don't like feeling this way, I thought after a few minutes.

I pushed the treadmill higher again.

If I don't have Tom to think about, I have to deal with my real life. I squeezed the tears back into my eyes.

I don't know how we're going to come up with the money this month to pay the bills. Jack and I can't even have a conversation without fighting. I feel so stressed out at home that I'm afraid I'll start eating again and gain back the weight I've lost.

I held onto the sides of the treadmill, feeling my heart start racing again.

I need my fantasy, I realized. *Since I made it up, I might as well make it work for me.*

I closed my eyes, holding tighter to the treadmill so I didn't fall.

Let's see.... OK, Tom loves me, he just doesn't know how to show it. My heart started slowing and the ache in my stomach eased a little.

We are soul mates and meant to be together. I just have to be patient.

My arms and shoulders started feeling lighter.

I can make up anything I want.

I started jogging, feeling much better.

Am I just escaping? I asked myself.

Yes, I definitely am, but at least it won't make me fat or cause a hangover. So how bad could it be?

After a few weeks, though, I started feeling a little ridiculous. One day, doing my weights, I decided I needed to know if he felt anything for me. If not, I needed to get over this and deal with my real life. My back ached again. I plotted an ambush while closely watching Tom's movements. I saw him go into the locker room, knowing he would be leaving the gym in ten minutes. I grabbed my stuff and started stretching by the exit. When I saw him walking out, I followed him outside.

"Do you have a minute? I need some advice." I said.

"Sure, I'm not in a rush. What's going on?"

He stopped and leaned against the building with his arms folded. He looked at me, waiting.

How was I going to bring this up, I wondered?

"Well, remember a while ago I told you that my husband and I are more like roommates? Well, it's getting worse. We can't even talk to each other without fighting. I don't know what to do."

"I don't know what to tell you. I'm a little uncomfortable talking about this. I don't know if I would like my wife talking to someone else about our marriage." His cheeks became increasingly rose colored.

"Well, I don't mean to make you uncomfortable. I'm sorry I said something. Never mind." I picked up my bag and started walking away, feeling embarrassed.

"Wait. Come back," Tom said. He was still leaning outside the building but put his foot up on one of the car bumpers.

"All I can say is, my wife and I had a rough patch and we got through it. A few years ago, I was in a funk. I started having an affair and felt alive again. It lasted two years, but in the end, I realized my wife loved me, and we decided to work through it. It hasn't been easy, but I decided I want someone to grow old with."

"Was it hard?" I asked.

"Definitely. We had a lot to work out and used a counselor to help us. It got pretty ugly for a while."

"Are you happy about your decision?" I asked, watching his facial features closely.

"Yes." He kicked a rock on the sidewalk, looking down. "It's what I chose."

"Again, I don't mean to make you uncomfortable," I said. "It's just that I am so confused, and it helps me to hear about other people's experiences. I'm sorry."

"No, it's ok. If I can help you, I guess it's okay. It's not easy, but I know my wife loves me and I am committed to making things work," he said. "I am going to be faithful from now on," he added.

I felt nauseous and took a sip of water.

This is not about me. I can handle that he wants to be faithful. If he was going to stray, I'm sure it would be with me. I can respect his decision, I told myself.

"Well, that's very admirable," I said. "Good for you. I appreciate your honesty and thanks for listening to me."

"No problem," he said and went off towards his car.

My face filled with sadness. I watched him walk off. I walked to my car. I tried to convince myself that it was better to know the truth. He was admirable and devoted to his wife. This was a good thing. Now I could move on. So, was I still hot? All I could do was assume, "Yes!" He just wasn't in the market for additional love.

3 Oh, You're on the List

Again, the weeks went by and I enjoyed my friendship with Tom, trying to admire his devotion to his wife. One day I was walking across the weight room floor and saw Ernie talking to some friends. I walked over.

"Hilary, do you know each other? This is Claudio?" Ernie asked.

Oh, Claudio from the hot list. Hmm. Nice smile. Very tall.

"Oh," I said out loud. "I'm surprised I've never met you before."

"Well, I tried to say 'hi' to you once, but you just kind of grunted at me," Claudio said.

Very white teeth, I thought.

"How embarrassing," I said. "I'm sorry. I must have been in the zone and not heard you."

We started walking and ended up next to each on the cardio machines. He told me he was married and had two children and we compared what it was like having teens at home. As he was talking, I noticed his tall, lanky build. He wore long pants and shirt, but you could see the outline of his very fit body underneath. He had a beige skin tone and I figured, due to his name, that he was of either Spanish or Italian descent. I couldn't see his hair under his baseball cap.

What did he tell Ernie to get himself on the list?" I wondered.

The weeks went by. Claudio and I talked in passing and whenever we were in the same area. He ran, and sometimes I would find myself on the machine next to him. It was very pleasant.

4 Red Haired Girl

More weeks went by. One day, in the section of the gym with a good view of the guys doing weights, my legs were flying back and forth on the elliptical, keeping time to a very fast remix of Journey's *Don't Stop Believing*. The machine was bouncing as my legs worked hard to stay with the beat.

Who needs guys anyway? I thought.

I wiped the sweat out of my eyes and checked my pulse.
I was doing great. My heartbeat was up. And I was over Tom.

So what if my feelings had been out of control? Hopefully, he never knew, and I respected that he was trying to make his marriage work. It wasn't a personal rejection, so I didn't have to wonder what I did wrong. It wasn't about me. I didn't have to feel bad about myself. I could just let it go.

There have to be other things I can think about besides men. There's work, the kids, getting in shape, the house... Hmmm, there's Claudio walking by heading to his treadmill. My he looked hot.

He tipped his hat and gave me a sexy smile. I tilted my head to the right and smiled.

So much for forgetting guys.

Just then, Kathy, a girl I had met through Tom, got on the elliptical next to me. We exchanged greetings and I turned my music down so I could hear her.

Tom walked by on his way to the weight section. "I saw him having breakfast at Whole Foods the other day," she said, nodding towards him.

"Really?" I asked, as my chest tightened a little.

"He was with a red-haired girl."

I felt like I couldn't breathe. I was startled by my dramatic response.

He never asked me to breakfast. He never asked me to go anywhere out of the gym. How could this be?

"Are you sure it was him?" I asked.

Who was she? He's supposed to be LOYAL.

"Maybe it was his wife," I said, trying to hear over the loud heartbeat pulsing in my ears.

"I don't know. I've never met her."

The next day Kathy called me while I was working.

"I ran into Tom and the same girl again at Whole Foods. I walked up and said hi. They looked very cozy. He introduced me to her. Then, she turned to me and said, 'And I am not his wife.' Why would she say that?"

"Oh my God, someone must have heard us," I said. "Who was near us that day? How embarrassing."

We tried to figure out who the spy was. Selfishly I was only concerned about one thing.

"If she wasn't his wife, did she say what their relationship was?" I asked.

"No." she said.

The next day Kathy and I were back on the elliptical. "There she is," she said.

"Where?"

"Over there with the red hair."

I scanned the area.

That girl? With the frizzy red hair and not so small butt? He picked her over me?

"Her?" I said out loud. "Maybe she is a friend of the family."

We watched her and Tom talking. I started feeling sick again.

Maybe there's a logical explanation. Don't jump to conclusions, I kept telling myself. *But he was supposed to be faithful to his wife. It's supposed to be me* kept repeating itself over and over in my mind.

As the days went by, I watched them more and more. And I kept feeling worse. Even though it made no sense, Tom was married and so was I. Yet, somehow, I needed to think that I would have been his first choice after his wife.

Otherwise I didn't matter. Otherwise I was irrelevant.

If I let go of the fantasy, I started feeling panicked. It was a horrible feeling. For some reason, I needed to think that someone wanted me. It kept me from sinking to the other side and starting to eat again.

The fantasy was a construct in my mind that kept me going. It filled a missing piece for me. It quieted the *I don't matter* and *I'm not okay the way I am* voice in my head. I didn't have to experience the pain of feeling that they might be true.

To make myself feel better, I searched for Claudio, finding him easily with either his signature yellow or bright green hat. I walked over to him and flirted, laughing dramatically and acting like I was having a great time, hoping to make Tom jealous.

As if he cares, I thought.

But I had to do something to ease my chronic jealousy and panic.

5 You Made my Day

One day Claudio was on the treadmill. I got on the elliptical right next to him.

"I'm tired of this music," I said. I took out my earbuds.

"I don't know how to get new songs. My kids have gotten me the ones I have, but I hate being dependent on them for new ones."

"I use something on the internet to get running music," he said as he ran. "When I remember the name, I can help you."

"Great," I said. "I would love that. See you later. I'm going to do weights."

I walked toward the front of the gym.

FINDING THE OLD HILARY AGAIN

Oh shit, I thought. *There's Jack, my husband. He rarely shows up at the gym. Why did he come now? He must have had a sixth sense. Thank God, I wasn't flirting with Claudio when he saw me.*

"Hi," I said. "I'm about to do weights."

He kept looking around to see who was paying attention to me.

"Can I do them with you?" Jack asked.

Ugh, does he have to? I thought.

I sort of nodded my head yes. I walked over to the free weights and started doing some arm exercises. Jack started to follow me, looking around to see who was there. He nodded to Tom and they exchanged greetings. He waved to a few people and stopped to talk to them. I kept doing the weights. Jack came and did a few sets in between his schmoozing with people he knew.

He's not even working out, I thought. *Why did he even come here? Is he just here to check on me? This is the one place I can be happy and be myself,* I thought. *Why does he have to come and ruin it? I don't even think he's a member anymore. He must have just walked in like he owned the place.*

I continued to do my weights.

Shouldn't I be happy that my husband is here? For years I've been complaining about him not wanting to spend time with me yet here he is and all I want to do is run away.

After I finished my "express workout" where I hit all body parts in a half hour, I told Jack I'd be home after I stretched.

"OK, I think I'll just head out," he said. "See you at home."

I went into the corner and grabbed a mat to stretch on. I closed my eyes.

How come no one talked to me when Jack was here? It was so NOT fun. I felt like a prisoner with my warden.

Ernie saw me as I got up.

"Did you see that?" I asked. "I don't know why I hate it so much when he is around."

"He was peeing on his territory."

"You think?" I asked. I couldn't help looking around for a glimpse of Tom and "The Girl".

"You are such a different person around him," Ernie said. "You're like a zombie."

I am? I know I feel different, but I didn't know it was that obvious.

"Really? Can you tell?"

"Oh my God. He has ruined you. You are not the same fun, outgoing wonderful Hilary that I knew in high school. When are you going to leave him?"

Leave him?

It was the second time Ernie had mentioned leaving. Even though I had been dissatisfied and virtually alone in my relationship for years, I hadn't ever really considered leaving. I think I secretly nursed a small hope that we could work things out.

Even though I constantly complained about having no relationship, no money and no sex, Ernie's question shook me up.

Cold as it may seem, I wasn't making enough money to support myself. And even if I could, where would I go? What about the kids? I never thought I would ever think about divorce. That's just not me. Would I want to be single? I hated dating. Ugh. What would I wear? Would I need plastic surgery on my wrinkles? A boob lift? What about my varicose veins?

I started walking out, still muttering to myself, feeling more and more dejected as I walked to my car.

"What is that?" I said out loud. I scrunched up my eyes and face, trying to see what was stuck in my door handle. I broke into a grin as I looked at it.

"Podcast" was written on Claudio's business card. My depression was immediately replaced with a surge of happiness.

I emailed Claudio as soon as I got home. "Thanks for making my day." I wrote.

He asked if we could text instead of email since he was at work and he was afraid that his company monitored his emails. I gave him my number.

"So how did I make your day," he texted.

"Too much to text. Tell you tomorrow."

"OK," followed by a strange symbol.

"What is that?" I asked.

"Kisses," he said.

Uh-oh, I thought. *Kisses? Am I ready for this? This is way more than my fantasy relationship with Tom. This might just be crossing the line. I didn't answer the text but instead couldn't help wondering what I was getting myself into.*

6   I'm Your Type?

The next day at the gym, I told Claudio that his card on my car had made my day since I had been upset about Jack being at the gym.

"That's it? Oh," he said, smile disappearing. "Ok." He started walking away.

I ran after him and grabbed his arm, turning him to face me. "Did I say something wrong?"

"No, I was just expecting something else, I guess," he said.

"Well, you'll have to tell me later since I have to run to get my daughter from the bus." I grabbed my stuff and walked out.

Later that afternoon my phone rang.

"I was hoping you were excited because you had some sort of interest in me," he said.

Interest? I thought. *Huh? He's married.*

"What kind of interest?" I asked.

"I've been watching you for a while," he said.

Watching me? Fat Hilary in the corner? You've got to be kidding, I thought.

"Your body was made for sex," he continued.

Me? Made for sex?

I bit my lip to keep myself from laughing out loud.

"It was?" I asked.

"No one has told you that before?" he asked.

"No, not me…not ever."

He had to get off the phone because someone walked into his office.

123

FINDING THE OLD HILARY AGAIN

Did he really just say that?

That's not what Jack had told me the week before we got married 17 years earlier. He had been driving me to work on the Wednesday morning before our Sunday wedding. He turned off Third Avenue onto 56th street.

"You know, you are not my type. That's not why I'm marrying you," he said.

"What do you mean I'm not your type?" I asked.

"I've always been attracted to a different kind of woman."

We had just arrived in front of my building and we were blocking traffic. The beeping cars were making me anxious.

"Well, okay. I gotta go into work. Talk to ya later."

I got out of the car and headed into work.

He's just scared, I thought, *second marriage and all. It's normal to push away the person you love. I'm sure that's what most people do the week before they get married. I'm sure it's normal.*

I became distracted at work and didn't have a chance to dwell on it until our honeymoon in Italy. Jack was staring at a woman who was walking by. His mouth was open in amazement.

"Is that your type?" I tried to keep my tone neutral.

"Yes," he said. "See the flowing skirt and how it moves when she walks. I am wondering what she has underneath that."

The anger I felt covered up my hurt.

This was our honeymoon. How could he be looking at someone else like that?

I couldn't stand it. But, instead of telling him it bothered me, I blurted out, "well, she probably has razor blades in her vagina. That would probably hurt."

124

Where did that come from? I wondered.

"Really?" His expression was that of a little boy.

I could see he was thinking about it.

Good, I thought. *Think about that.*

Much later, when I was calmer, I asked him more about his type. He loved a feminine woman who wore flowing skirts, high heels, and monochromatic outfits. She was a real girly girl and had perfect hair and a closet full of feminine shoes to choose from.

Instead of high heels in my shoe rack, I had sneakers—running, aerobics, cross trainers. I was a jeans and sweatshirt, run out with your hair wet, kind of girl. I didn't pay much attention to my clothing and loved my comfortable cotton underwear and support bras. For years Jack tried to turn me into "his type," giving me gift certificates to Victoria's Secret and trying to hire personal shoppers to "help" me. But none of it ever made him look at me like he looked at that woman.

I suppose someone else would have seen the signs and fled. But not me. I was 34, late for work, and thinking about everything I needed to do before the wedding. I assumed that when you got married, you had great sex and your husband found you attractive. Why would I worry about a little comment like that?

Jack's sexual rejection over the next 17 years left me feeling very undesirable and unattractive. On top of that, I felt stupid for ignoring yet another sign before our wedding.

The next day I called Claudio. I figured if he could talk so intimately, I could be honest with him.

"Your comments caused me to go down a very disturbing memory lane. My husband says he is not attracted to me and it doesn't occur for him to have sex with me. We haven't had any in years. I'm so used to feeling bad about myself that this is coming as a shock. You sure this isn't a joke?"

"No, I think you are hot and sexy. I've been wanting to approach you but your growl kind of put me off."

"That again? Sorry. But seriously? Aren't my butt and legs way too big?"

"Not at all. I love the way you look."

"Get out of here. I know I'm athletic, but when did big butts get attractive?"

"Well, I've always liked them."

I can't believe this, I thought. *When did this change? Growing up we all wanted to look like Twiggy.*

She was a very thin model in the 60's who wore bright colors and had long eyelashes. My sister was naturally thin, but not me. My father's favorite phrase was "you can never be too rich or too thin."

Claudio's comments were shocking to me.

"I wish I had known that a man could actually love a larger butt. My entire life would have been different," I said. "I wouldn't have hated the way I looked all these years."

"Well, would you like to go out for a drink tonight? We could discuss it some more."

Uh-oh. I thought.

"I would, but I have to get back to pick up my daughter. Maybe another time," I said.

"Okay, see you tomorrow," I said, but he had already hung up.

That was abrupt, I thought.

I hung up the phone and took a deep breath.

Did I want to? I didn't know. It was one thing to flirt and have emotional affairs, but to have a date? That seemed like crossing the line. Time to cool things down with this guy, I thought. I'm not sure what he's about. This is wrong and very dangerous.

For the next few days, however, the phrase "made for sex" kept repeating itself over and over in my head. As it did, the excitement of being desired filled me with that same drug-like euphoria. Could something that feels this good be bad?

7 Hurricane Irene – August 24, 2011

For the next few weeks, despite Claudio's attention, I kept watching Tom and The Girl. Maybe she was a family friend. Maybe she knew his wife and they were all just good friends.

During Hurricane Irene, our shoreline neighborhood was evacuated. Jack, Jesse, Haley and I left our house late Saturday and temporarily moved into my parents' house. The gym was closed on Sunday, but Monday morning, I braved the fallen trees to get there. Kathy, my new friend, was there as well and joined me on the ellipticals near the front door. In mid-sentence, she hit me.

"Look at that," she said.

"What?" I asked.

"There's Tom and The Girl walking in together. He's carrying her stuff."

Why would they be coming in together? Did they spend the night together? Is his wife away? What did this mean?

I watched them go into their respective locker rooms and then circle back to find each other. Tom was not acting normal. He was giddy and laughing. He went to do weights and she got on the treadmill. He kept coming back over to her and talking to her. He seemed to be laughing nervously.

Kathy chattered on, but I tuned her out, conscious of the pain in my stomach. I couldn't stand to watch this anymore. The pain was getting worse. I needed to get away and I couldn't say anything to Kathy since she didn't know how I felt about Tom.

"Gotta go," I said, grabbing my stuff and walking away.

I headed over to the middle section of cardio equipment. I got on an elliptical in the back row. My chest felt so much pressure I couldn't breathe. I moved my arms slowly.

It was supposed to be me! played on an infinite loop in my brain. *Maybe she didn't have kids. Maybe she wasn't married, and it was easier. Maybe she threw herself at him and he just said yes.*

I felt the pressure in my throat from trying not to cry.

I had respected him because he was being faithful. What a fucking joke. Well, I guess once you cheat, you cheat again.

I looked at her back flab showing out of her tight shirt.

That? I thought. *You can have her.*

I saw Claudio out of the corner of my eye but didn't go over to him. I didn't have the energy to pretend to be happy. I finished my workout and walked to my car. I circled the parking lot where I knew Tom parked. There was his blue Ford station wagon next to The Girl's large black SUV. How cute. She parked right next to him.

My phone rang. It was my little sister in North Carolina.

"How are you faring the hurricane?" she asked.

I could barely focus on what she was saying.

"Umm, fine, we're making do. I can't believe the guy I have a major crush on is hanging out with The Girl."

"What?" She said, not knowing what I was talking about.

"I feel sick," I said.

"Well, take Vitamin C. That's what Mom always says."

"Yes, thanks. How are you doing?"

I didn't even hear her answer. I wasn't aware of driving home, but somehow my car pulled into my parents' driveway. I had really believed him. It physically hurt.

What was I going to do? I couldn't talk to anyone about it. I felt like I was going crazy.

Before I walked in, I saw a text from Claudio.

"Are you mad at me? Why didn't you say hello?"

"No," I texted back. "Maybe we can have that drink soon."

"I'd like that," he said.

Thank God for Claudio, I thought.

The attention was like salve on a wound. It made the painful images of Tom giggling next to The Girl hurt just a little bit less.

8 Salve on the Wound

For the next few weeks, I sought out Claudio at the gym. I felt like my world had been rocked. I could handle Tom's lack of interest by telling myself that he was devoted to his wife. What I couldn't deal with was that he hadn't chosen me. It felt like a stab in the heart.

What had kept me going was thinking that if he was going to fool around, it would be me. Crazy as it sounds, it made me feel like I mattered. I wasn't irrelevant for once. Even though it made no sense, I felt like a real person again. I can't really explain it any better. All I know is that it had kept me going and helped me ignore my situation at home.

But today, I felt stupid. I should never have believed Tom. He said he was going to be faithful. And I had thought that was honorable. Silly me. Fooled again. I was lied to and left in the driveway once again.

Claudio's attention kept me from sinking into the very dark place where Fat Hilary had lived for so many years. I tried to tell myself I was no longer Fat Hilary. I wasn't that girl being left behind. I felt like I was holding on to the edge of a cliff and trying not to fall off.

On three different occasions Claudio asked me to go out for drinks, but each time circumstances outside my control got in the way.

"I'm done chasing you," Claudio said after the third time. "If you want to get together, you ask me. I'm not going to pursue you anymore. It seems like I am trying to force things. I'll just see you at the gym." And he hung up the phone.

Wait, I thought, staring at the phone in my hand. I was sitting in my car about to walk into a client's office. *You think I'm hot. How can you give up on me that easily? It was circumstances. It wasn't my fault. What if he was the only guy that would ever be attracted to me ever again? WAIT!* I screamed inside my head.

I might never feel special and attractive again. I can't let him run away now. He can't run away now. I loved this feeling of being pursued. WAIT! My brain kept screaming.

Get a grip, I told myself.

I walked into the client meeting.

I couldn't turn off the voice of Fat Hilary in my head.

Did you really think he was interested? Who are you kidding? If you're that easy to give up on, do you think he really cared?

I couldn't stand listening to her voice. I was determined to make something happen. That week my daughter had a two-hour tumbling class. I called Claudio and told him I had two hours free.

We arranged to meet at a local restaurant. He was already there when I arrived. I stared at him. I had never seen him without his hat. He had very short, tight curls. He looked like a different person. Plus, he was dressed in a very nice blue suit. The shirt was starched and unwrinkled even after a full day's work. We said hi and I giggled like a schoolgirl. We walked into the bar.

We sat at a small table for two. After the first glass of merlot I started to relax. We discussed work. He worked at an accounting firm. He ordered a steak and I ordered a small Caesar salad. I was too nervous to eat anything else.

Claudio seemed relaxed. He told me several stories about his work. He did not seem rushed and seemed to be enjoying telling me his stories.

I looked at my watch. "I have to go," I said.

"Ok, let me get the bill," he said.

He paid with cash.

Interesting. This way there was no trail. I wonder if he has done this before.

We walked out and stood at my car.

"Ok, thanks," I said. He gave me an awkward kiss and walked away.

I drove home telling myself I didn't do anything wrong. We were talking business and just had a drink and a bite to eat. Plus, we parted with just a peck on the cheek and a one-handed hug. Like good friends, right?

After that, things were uncomfortable. He didn't text me and wasn't coming up to me at the gym like he had been. I couldn't understand what had happened. The anxiety of wondering was exhausting me.

I called Claudio one day. "How come you are not all over me like you were? Why did you back off?"

"You gave me no signals when we were out that you were interested in anything more. It's up to you if you want more from me."

What kind of signals was I supposed to give? We had an enjoyable friendly dinner. He certainly didn't act like he wanted more. What was I supposed to do? Jump on him? That's just not my style. Now it's up to me? I'm confused. I don't need this, I thought. *I don't even like him that much. He sort of looked funny without his hat. I should probably just let the whole thing go. Back away. Stay faithful physically. So, I had one date. So what? It was practically a business dinner.*

Do I really want to do that? I argued with myself. *This may be the last time someone is interested in me. He seemed to want something. Can I afford to ignore this? Do I want to live an entirely sex-less life? This might be my last chance.*

The constant argument in my head was unbearable. One weekend Jack was away. Haley was with me but was going tumbling on Saturday morning.

"Are you free?" I texted Claudio.

"Yes," he said.

"Meet me at my house at noon." I gave him my address. He said ok.

"Are you squeamish about blood?" I texted him later after obsessing for an hour about whether to say anything about my time of the month. I didn't want to have to say it in person.

"Yes."

I called him and asked if he still wanted to come over. He understood I was out of commission. I met him at my house, and we talked. He told me that his parents were black.

"Why are you so light?" I asked.

"My mother was much lighter. My father was very, very dark."

At some point, we were in the kitchen. It was extremely awkward. I could see the outline of his hard-on.

Oh my God! I thought.

"Do you want to see it?" he asked.

"I guess," I said.

He took his penis out of his elastic waist pants. I didn't know what to do. I couldn't speak. He asked if I wanted to touch it. I just stood there and felt like I was five years old.

Did I want to?

I just stared at it. It had been a long time since I saw a penis that big and that hard, and this one definitely was.

I pulled my eyes away and looked at the clock. "Uh oh, I have to go get Haley."

"Yes, you need to do that."

"Sorry," I said.

"I'm a patient man."

He put his penis back into his underwear and pulled his pants back in place.

9   Am I Torn?

The next few weeks were filled with an excited feeling of anticipation. I could sense when Claudio arrived at the gym. I confirmed it when I could see his baseball cap showing above the other heads. We exchanged knowing looks and sexual innuendoes. But he didn't suggest getting together again. It started to bother me.

Was I not attractive anymore? What was wrong with me? Did I do something wrong? I finally asked him why.

"I told you this is up to you. I am not going to pressure you since you are obviously torn."

Am I torn? I asked myself. *Is this what I really want? Do I really want to cross that line? Once I am unfaithful, the dam would be broken. What would prevent me from acting this way again? Do I want to be labeled as the kind of woman who cheats on her husband?* I didn't think so.

But, despite these thoughts, the image of his hard penis stayed with me as I went through my day. I felt like a sex-deprived 18-year-old boy. I couldn't stop thinking about it. I felt completely out of control.

Finally, one Friday night, I dropped Haley off at her cheerleading practice and called him.

"Meet me at my office," I said.

"Ok, I'll get some wine. Maybe that will loosen you up a little," he said.

I had on my going-out outfit in anticipation—tight black jeans and maroon sweater over my push up bra. I got to the office first. When I let him in, I saw him smile and nod his head, pleased at what he saw.

We went into the conference room and opened the bottle. We talked as if we were business associates. Finally, I asked him if he wanted to see my office. Sure, he said, white teeth showing in his sensual smile.

I took him in, and we shut the door. I was ready and was no longer concerned about my infidelity. I was ready to cross the line. I couldn't wait to get that hard penis where nothing hard had been for so long.

He sat down in my swivel chair. I straddled him, but my tight jeans did not allow much movement.

"How do I do this?" I asked, feeling stupid.

"Just take off one leg," he said. I pulled off one leg of the pants and my underwear as well. I straddled him, feeling that long, hard cock inside me.

"Oh," I murmured, "That feels so good. It's been so long."

My words were interrupted by the door opening. Claudio backed the swivel chair into the door, slamming it shut, practically smashing the hand of the cleaning lady. I think she got the message because she didn't clean my office that weekend.

"Where were we?" I asked, heart pounding from the relief that it wasn't my boss trying to get in the door. I took a second to calm down and then straddled him again, about to groan when the phone rang. I looked to see who it was.

"It's Haley."

"You have to get it."

"Mom! Where are you? We got done early and I am the last one here. Why aren't you here? Please come. The coaches are waiting with me, but they want to go."

"I'll be right there," I said.

"No problem, he said. "We'll have other chances."

Oh my God, I groaned, feeling almost a physical ache. I felt like a guy—I had sex on the brain at all times.

FINDING THE OLD HILARY AGAIN

Two days later, on Sunday, I got a text from him.

"Meet me at Exit 9 at 3:00."

When I got to Exit 9, I looked for the bar he was at. No bars in sight. I texted him. "Where are you?"

"Room 216."

"Huh?"

"Room 216 at the Exit 9 motel."

Holy shit. I didn't have time to think about how I felt about this. I found the motel and knocked on the door of room 216. Claudio opened it, buck naked. I couldn't even look at him. I couldn't move.

"Take off your clothes. What are you waiting for?"

My arms would not move. I stood there looking at him. I was trying to get him to see that I needed help, but he was just looking at me like I was crazy.

"I am frozen," I whispered. "I really can't move. You have to help me."

He helped me undress and we attempted to have sex. He lost the condom and had to get another one.

Is this right? I thought. *What am I supposed to be doing? Am I any good?* I wondered.

I couldn't relax and finally gave up on myself.

I helped him to climax and then he got his clothes on.

He looked at his phone. "Gotta go."

He practically ran to his car.

I yelled across the parking lot. "Did I do something wrong? What happened?"

"Shush. Someone might see us. I have to go." He got in his car and drove off.

"You weren't worried about that five minutes ago," I muttered.

I got into my car and hurried to catch up to him. My heart was racing. I pulled up alongside him. He was focused on driving and didn't see me.

Was I horrible? Is that it?

I was so nervous. I wondered if I'd get a second chance. The pressure in my chest felt terrible. Breathe, I told myself. Breathe.

I drove the rest of the way home feeling sick. What did I do? Someone else might have been concerned that they had broken their marriage vows, but not me. As far as I was concerned, my marriage vows had been broken when my husband checked out of our marriage both physically and emotionally years before.

Was I justifying my actions and blaming Jack? Yes, but my marriage was not on my mind. The only thing I was thinking about was would I get a second chance to be with Claudio. It had felt so good to have him want me and desire me. Knowing I caused that penis to get that hard made me feel like a woman again. And I hadn't felt that way for a long, long time. I didn't want to give that feeling up.

The next few days, I didn't hear from him. I watched my phone for texts all day. Fat Hilary was all over me.

"See, you were horrible. No wonder Jack didn't want to have sex with you. You better stay in this marriage. You can't even have an affair."

I started feeling depressed and apathetic. I was irritable around the kids and noticed that I was eating and drinking more than I had been. I got on the scale. I was up three pounds. I had to get over this. I needed to know what happened.

I called Claudio from my driveway. I told him how insecure I was feeling and didn't understand why he had pursued me so heavily and now was not even calling.

"Hey, I told you we'll get together when we can. I'm busy this week."

"Did I do something wrong?" I asked, hating myself for sounding so pathetic but needing to know.

"No."

"Then why were you all over me before? I don't get it."

"I said we'd get together when we can. It's not a big deal."

But it was a big deal for me, I thought. *I loved when he was pursuing me. I wondered if the thrill of the chase was gone for him. He had had me and now the tides had turned. I was no longer in control.*

I hated the feeling. My head felt like it was going to explode. I thought I just wanted sex, but it wasn't worth feeling so needy and pathetic for someone I didn't even really like. What's the point of a nice hard dick if I was too nervous and uncomfortable to get satisfied myself?

But I didn't say no. Every few weeks we would get together, and he even bought me a purple vibrator, trying to get me to come. We would have dinner and make out in his car, with him getting relief and me not. I just wasn't orgasming. But even so, I didn't stop seeing him because the feeling of being desired was like a drug. I was addicted. Without his attention, I crashed, became depressed, had no energy, and lived only for the moment when I would hear from him again.

10 Obsessing

A few weeks later I was sitting in my car outside a client's office. I was fifteen minutes early for my appointment to set up the dates of our employee benefits presentation. I was driving myself crazy looking at my phone, willing it to show a text from Claudio. I had not heard from him since I had last seen him a week before. He hadn't even been at the gym. I felt nervous and my stomach hurt.

I looked at my phone again. Nothing.

Should I text him? Or wait? I could text him to see if he's ok. Or, should I not and pretend I don't care. I just didn't know what to do.

I closed my eyes and felt the heat of the October sun coming in through my sunroof. Would it really matter five years from now if Claudio texted me today? I asked myself.

I didn't even really like him. His stories were boring, and he told them in too much detail. Why was I letting him affect my life like this? It made no sense.

I checked my phone—still no text. Back in my single days we called it "obsessing" or "freaking out."

One memory of this stood out. It was December 1991 when I was single. I had gone to a spa out west. I went alone over Christmas vacation, using money I had won in a lawsuit when I was injured skiing. I loved it there—the early morning walks, hourly exercise classes, healthy food, and massages were part of the package. I was in heaven and felt great physically.

One of the things they offered was something called a lifestyle analysis. I scheduled one, not having any idea what it was. I walked into a little room where a man invited me to sit down.

"Do you have any concerns?" he asked.

FINDING THE OLD HILARY AGAIN

"Not really," I said. "My life is fine. Everything's good."

He nodded his head.

Why is he looking at me that way? Am I supposed to have a problem? Let me see if I can find one for him, I thought.

"OK, well, there's something strange that I am doing that I don't really understand. I am obsessing about which leotard to wear every day. I am driving myself crazy. I know it's not that important, but I can't stop worrying every morning when I have to choose. It seems like my life depends on this decision."

"Well, is anything wrong? How's work?"

"Fine."

"How are your relationships?"

"Fine." I sat there quietly for about a minute.

"Well, actually, not fine if I really think about it." My head started hurting and I rubbed my temples.

"Oh my God. I'm in a relationship with a man who had told me he was divorced. Later I found out he was still married. It sounds a little crazy, but the reason he didn't leave his wife was because he has a chronic disease. He told me that if he felt better by January 1st, he was going to leave her, and we could be together. But, it's almost New Years and he's not feeling better. I guess he's going to stay where he is."

The analyst handed me a tissue. I continued. "I guess I either stay as the other woman and never have a real relationship or I say goodbye and lose the only man I have ever really loved. It's a lose-lose."

I stopped to think. "I have no good alternative. There is not going to be a happy ending."

He handed me some more tissues as the reality of my situation hit me.

We discussed how obsessing about the leotards was a way of denying that I had a difficult decision to make. The floodgates opened, and I couldn't stop crying, not just that day, but for the next five days, even after I got home. I looked like a mess, but it felt good to be able to let my feelings out instead of ignoring them. I didn't have an answer, but I was no longer hung up on leotards. It took me another four months and the Landmark Forum, to finally get the courage to end that relationship.

Coming back to the present in my car, I asked myself, *what is the issue here?*

Oh, my real life.

I shut my eyes so the tears could not escape. I couldn't go into my client's office looking puffy.

It's a lot easier to deal with whether Claudio will text or not than to really look at what I am doing and how my life is going. I am having an affair, my marriage does not work, my finances are not where I want them to be, and I am doing badly at work. I don't know how to fix any of these, so it's a lot easier to focus on Claudio.

I discovered there was another piece as well while I sat there feeling like Fat Hilary.

I know why I'm obsessing, but why do I automatically feel unattractive and pathetic if I don't hear from Claudio. I only feel good when he pays attention to me. Why is that? Why does he have this power over me? Why do I need him, an obvious sleazebag, to validate me? Why can't I just do that myself and feel good regardless?

All I had to do was tell myself I was fine by myself. I didn't need him. I took a deep breath and looked at the clock. Three minutes until my meeting. Good. I was over him. I started getting my papers together.

My phone beeped. "What's up?" the text said. It was from Claudio. My body surged with elation. I could feel the drug-like euphoria flow through my body.

He still wants me, I thought. *I am still hot and sexy.*

We arranged to meet that night for drinks. I breathed deeply, enjoying the wonderful feeling.

And the see-saw continued. In between our get-togethers, I would try to talk myself out of my anxiety by writing in a journal. It helped me get through our non-texting periods. I wrote about my insecurity, worry and doubts, as well as Claudio's black penis and what I wanted him to do with it. I was careful to close my computer down and put it away at night just in case Jack got curious and wanted to know what I was typing.

11 He Read the Journal

One night at 2:00 AM I was awakened by the terse words, "Get up!"

I looked up. Jack was standing over me. I was about to say, "I've told you a thousand times not to wake me up from a sound sleep," until I saw his I-will-kill-you eyes.

I closed my eyes and pretended I was still sleeping.

"I know what you've been doing," he said.

Don't react, I told myself. *You don't know what he's talking about.*

"What?" I asked, opening one eye.

"You left your computer open and I read the whole thing. I know what you've been thinking, fantasizing and doing."

"Oh," I said. I felt the damp perimenopausal sweat on my sheets.

Think! I silently yelled at myself.

Let's see, last night I was typing on my journal. I looked up at the movie Haley was watching. Engrossed, I went to sit with her on the couch to watch the rest. I must have left my computer open. Oh, shit.

"What have you got to say for yourself?" he asked, glaring at me, controlled fury shaking his voice.

I stared him straight in the eyes.

Go for it, I told myself. *This is your moment to be real.*

I took a deep breath and was suddenly wide awake.

"I'm sorry if it hurts you," I said, "but I won't apologize for the truth. I have been telling you for years that we have no relationship, no sex life or physical contact, and that our finances stress me out. You have ignored me. I was feeling really bad about myself. Someone started paying attention to me, and I liked how it made me feel."

"You cannot have these thoughts and still honor our marriage."

"Oh, please. We are housemates, parents of the same children, and business partners. We have not had a real marriage for years."

"You have broken your vows." he said.

"Let's not talk about breaking vows, Mr. Let's-have-an-extraordinary-relationship who checked out of the marriage a long time ago."

"Are you saying what you did is my fault?"

"I am responsible for what I did, but you have ignored me. I tried everything to get your attention—relationship books, marriage workshops, love languages, sexy underwear—and nothing worked."

I pressed my teeth together so that I wouldn't start crying. "I finally gave up. I am tired of feeling bad about this."

"You are always upset about something. Did you know that?"

"That is so not true. I was happy before I got married. I had a great life."

"Well, you're the angriest person I know."

"I was never angry before I got married."

"So, again, you're saying all of this is my fault?"

"I'm saying this marriage isn't working for me."

"Well, if you have a new relationship with someone else, you're bringing yourself with you. You're gonna have the same problems in the next relationship. What do you think will be different?"

I bit my lip again.

Hang in there, I told myself.

I watched the minutes until my morning alarm went off at five a.m. I jumped up, grabbed my clothes, and went into the bathroom.

I was putting on my make-up when Jack pushed the door open. "Typical. Run to your gym boys," he said. "How come you take time to look good for them and not for me?"

This again?

I stayed silent. I finished putting on my mascara. I grabbed my bag and mumbled, "Because they pay attention to me." I headed down the stairs.

He followed me, glaring. "I don't suppose you could skip a day at the gym to finish talking about this," he said.

"No. We can talk later," I said. I opened the door and ran to my car.

At the gym, I rushed to an elliptical in the middle row, desperate to work off some of my anxiety. About 20 minutes later, Claudio came in and got on the treadmill in front of me. Desperate for some sympathy, I jumped down, hitting myself in the eye with the handle of the machine next to me. Ignoring the pain, I got on the treadmill next to him, and put my hand on his arm.

"Hi," he said with a gleam in his eye until he looked at my frantic eyes. "Uh oh, what's wrong?"

I moved closer to him so I could whisper into his ear. "My husband read my journal. He knows everything. I am freaking out."

He looked at me, mouth and eyes wide open. He pounded the treadmill with his fist. "You idiot. Why would you ever put any of this in writing?"

Stunned, I bit my lip so I wouldn't start crying. Without thinking, I turned on the treadmill and it started moving. "I've always kept a journal." I said with my head down. "It helps me work things out when I'm stressed."

"Does he know who I am?" he asked.

"No, I did not mention your name. You're safe. It's me who's fucked," I said.

"Idiot," he said again, staring at me with disgust. "Why would you do that?" He turned away, put on his earbuds, and broke into a full-length running stride.

Shocked at his dismissal, I stopped walking. The treadmill flung me off the back, throwing my body into the elliptical behind me. I rubbed my side. I whispered, "Because writing helped me deal …." I grabbed my stuff, crossed the room, and climbed the stairs to Fat Hilary's corner.

I made it seconds before the tears broke loose. My shoulders shook as my self-control crumbled. I looked for a tissue in my bag but couldn't find one. I avoided looking at the mirror to my right as I decided to make do with my towel.

I can't believe he is acting this way, I thought, feeling a sharp pain in my stomach.

The tears fell, releasing the stress of holding myself together all night.

Why am I more upset about Claudio than about Jack? I wondered.

FINDING THE OLD HILARY AGAIN

I was surprised to feel relieved that Jack had found out.

Maybe he'll kick me out and I won't be the one having to make the decision to leave. Or, he'll wake up and realize I am serious about the breakdown of our marriage and start listening to me.

Do I feel bad about what I've done? I asked myself. No. Absolutely not.

I remembered a morning 15 years before. I had asked Jack if he wanted to have sex, and he refused, saying, "No, maybe tonight."

"But last night you said maybe in the morning. And the morning before that you said maybe that night. You just never want to," I said.

"It just doesn't occur for me to have sex with you."

"What the hell does that mean?" I asked.

"I don't really think about having sex with you. I'm not attracted to you. You're not my type."

I stopped asking, and I started eating. Fifteen years and 40 pounds later, I was feeling unwanted, undesirable, and resigned about ever feeling good about myself again.

That day, despite having lost twenty-five pounds and gotten in better shape, the pain of this rejection came right back to me.

Why am I still so upset?

I asked myself, forgetting that this had started with Jack reading my journal.

Because today Claudio was not telling me how hot and sexy I was. He was concerned with one thing—how his life would be affected by my mistake.

How could I have thought he cared about me? I asked myself.

I looked around the gym and was grateful that no one had spotted me in my corner.

I thought all I was missing from my life was sex. Having it with someone like Claudio didn't make me feel better at all. It made me feel like a piece of crap.

I left my stuff and walked to the locker room, head down so no one would see my puffy red eyes. I grabbed some tissues and headed back to my corner.

Dreading going home, I stayed at the gym as long as possible, hoping Jack would be gone by the time I got home.

12 Why Did You Do This?
(The morning after he read my journal)

When I got back from the gym, Jack's car was still in the driveway.

Shit! I thought.

Jack was leaning against the counter, arms crossed, and his expression was a mix of anger and hurt. I walked past him to get to the coffee pot. He grabbed my shoulders and turned me so that was I facing him.

"Why don't you tell me why you did this," he said.

"I did. I've told you a thousand times."

"I might be ready to listen this time."

"I've heard that before."

"Try me."

"OK," I said, turning away so I could pour myself a cup of coffee. I tasted it and spit it in the sink. "When was this made?"

"A few hours ago," he said.

"No wonder," I said, dumping it in the sink.

I started making a new pot as I talked. "Like I told you, we haven't had any physical contact in years. I was afraid that this was my last chance to ever have sex, so I took it."

"Did you enjoy it?"

"Not really. I was too nervous and uncomfortable."

He looked at me and his face seemed to soften.

"I never came, if that means anything to you," I said.

He kept looking at me. "Is sex really that important to you?" he asked.

"Yes. I don't want to live the rest of my life without it."

He stared at the coffee dripping into the pot. "Well, I've always wanted to have a fun sex life."

"Well, then what happened? Why did you check out of the marriage 15 years ago?" I asked.

"I don't know. I did it in my first marriage too. I don't know if I ever told you that one of my girlfriends ended up having an affair, also, and it was with one of my good friends."

I knew which one he meant. She did? Miss perfectly coiffed and dressed?

"I didn't know that. Why?" I said.

"Well, I guess I did the same thing with her. I stopped being interested in sex and wasn't home much."

"But she was your type—you were attracted to her."

"Well, I guess it didn't matter."

You have got to be kidding me, I thought.

"All these years I thought the reason you didn't want sex with me was because I wasn't your type. If you didn't want it with her either, then it wasn't me." A feeling of relief washed over my entire body.

"I blamed myself for so many years." I thought of Fat Hilary's shame, hiding in the corner on the elliptical.

If only I had known this before, I might have had a different life.

"Did you do this with other girls as well?" I asked him.

"Yes, I did if I really think about it. I think it's a pattern."

We each poured ourselves a new cup of coffee. As I was getting the skim milk out of the fridge, I heard him say, "I need to figure out why I do this. I don't want to ruin our marriage."

"Well, good luck with that," I said. "How?"

"I don't know, but I'm smart, right?" he asked.

"Yes, you are. I've never doubted your intelligence."

"Thank you," he said. "That means a lot."

A few days later, Jack and I were alone in our bedroom, about to get ready for work. The kids had already left for school, so we had the house to ourselves. I had just come out of the shower.

"Show me what you did with him," he said, guiding me toward the bed.

"Excuse me?" I said.

"You opened your legs for him, so do it for me."

He is angry—I'm glad he's human. And, it's kind of a turn on. "Really?" I asked.

"You said you wanted sex," he said. "Let's have it."

Could I enjoy sex with Jack? There wouldn't be any lying or sneaking—it might be easier. I could just borrow the passion I felt for Claudio.

"Just pretend you're with someone else if you have to," he said, watching me.

Was he reading my mind?

He pushed me down on the bed. "Fake it if you need to," he said. I didn't have to since he came so fast.

This is what I've been upset about not getting? I asked myself.

When Jack went into the shower, I went to my hiding place, got out my vibrator and satisfied myself. Who needs Jack anyway? My battery-operated boyfriend (B.O.B.) was my new best friend—does the job, doesn't argue, insult me or come too fast—and all it needs is charged batteries, and it's good to …

"I will work on this," Jack said, coming out of the shower.

"Huh?" I said. "Oh, ok." I pushed the vibrator under the sheets. I waited to put it away until he had gone downstairs. For some reason, I didn't want him to know about this. It was my little secret. Almost like when I used to sneak eat. It was a cross between being embarrassed and having a secret that he didn't know about. My little secret and a way of getting back at him in some way.

13 Too Dangerous

Later that day I was driving to a meeting.

Did I really want to work on things with Jack? It wasn't exciting or passionate like it was with Claudio—just making out with him was exciting. It could have been because it was forbidden or new or because he acted like he was attracted to me. Unlike Jack. I knew I had to have closure with Claudio, or I wouldn't be able to pay any attention to Jack. I have to do it now, I thought.

I grabbed my phone.

"Can you talk?" I texted. He called, and we made small talk until I blurted out.

"Are you ever going to want to get together with me again?"

"No," he said. "Too dangerous. I'd be afraid your husband would be following us and trying to figure out who I am."

"Okay," I said.

We hung up. I was disappointed, but I knew it was better this way. I drove a little bit. Would I ever feel passion and desire again?

I drove some more.

Get a grip, I told myself. *Real life isn't about feeling good. Don't screw everything up for a little excitement. Make your marriage work. It's the right thing to do.*

14 Go-To Guy

Later that week I was busy packing my food for the day before getting on the road. Jack stepped into my way as I was going to the refrigerator.

"I've been doing a lot of research. Are you excited about this?" he asked.

"I'm trying to be, but I feel like we've been down this road before."

"That's all part of the past." he said.

"What's different this time?"

"Why are you so negative? Look what you did. Why should I trust you?" he asked.

"Why don't you answer my question instead of turning this on me and making me defensive?"

"Because if you're still going to other guys to get your needs met, we have no hope for this marriage."

"If I go to them, it's because they understand me and accept me as I am."

"Well, I want you to stop. Otherwise they become your go-to guy instead of me. Talk to me instead."

"I don't want to talk to you. All you ever try to do is fix me. I just want to be able to be myself."

"Well, if I try to listen better will you have me be your go-to guy?"

Ugh. I didn't want to, but I wasn't ready to say it was over. We had been together for a long time and he was the father of my children. He was loyal and would come to family functions with me. But mostly, he hadn't given up on me. He was still here.

What if I didn't find someone else who could put up with my mood swings and neediness? What if I was suffering from the grass is always greener? What if he was really a great guy, I was really lucky to have him, and I just couldn't see it right now?

"Ok, I'll try," I said.

I didn't say I will, I just said I will try, I said to myself. *He never did tell me how this time would be any different.*

15 Lovely Lady

The next day at the gym I purposely kept my head down. I got on my elliptical and focused on my book, part 3 of Diana Gabaldon's *Outlander* series. I loved the relationship between Claire and Jamie. That's the kind of relationship I want to have—true love, lost without the other, great sex all the time, partners.

Can I have that with Jack? I wondered. *I'm not sure. Maybe I really can give up my other crushes and I can feel closer to Jack. I've got nothing to lose.*

I raised my head up. I slapped the handlebars on my elliptical. "Again?" I said out loud.

Claudio was talking to the same girl for the fourth day in a row. Who was she? I'd never seen her before. They walked to the treadmills. They started running next to each other deep in conversation. I couldn't believe it. He wasted no time.

For the next few days I watched in amazement as they ran, stretched, and did weights together. She was mesmerized by what he was saying. What was going on here? I had found his stories long and boring.

After a few more days I couldn't take it anymore.

"Glad to see you're getting some action," I texted Claudio.

"I don't know what you mean," he replied.

FINDING THE OLD HILARY AGAIN

"Yes, you do," I said.

Finally, he said, "Well, if you mean that lovely lady that I talk to, she is very nice. I can't believe I never noticed her before."

Unbelievable, I thought. *Why did it bother me? It's not like I wanted him back—so what was it?*

The next day at the gym she walked up to him again.

That's it, I thought. *I never walked up to him like that. I always waited for him to come to me. If he didn't, I would pretend I didn't see him, convinced things were over between us. I lived for his contact but was usually too insecure to be the first to initiate it.*

It was something I'd done my whole life. I would never act interested in a guy. My mother always told me, "If a guy knows you like him, he won't be interested anymore." My mind went back 20 years.

I was in a seminar and was determined to have a breakthrough in my relationships. I decided to interview guys I had dated. I called up a guy named Dan. We met playing tennis at an alumni outing for our Big 8 Accounting firm. I was in consulting, and he was in accounting, so we didn't know each other. We spent some time together in the city—he was fun, smart, ambitious, and Jewish. I developed a massive crush on him, but we never became more than friends.

When I called Dan for the interview, I asked him why things had never worked out between us.

"What? Seriously? I never knew you liked me."

"I was crazy about you."

"You always talked about other guys and never let me know. I had no idea."

I remember putting the phone down stunned. I had loved this guy—and I thought it was so obvious. I guess I had taken my mother's words to heart. I was so good at pretending I didn't like someone that I acted like I didn't care.

Coming back to lovely lady and Claudio, her mother probably never told her that. She was making it obvious that she liked him, and he was responding.

Could I ever have a guy that I felt so comfortable with that I could just assume he wanted me to be there? What would it be like to have a relationship with someone who enjoyed spending time with me?

I wanted to be secure enough to know I belonged and could just be myself instead of playing games.

I scrunched up my face. Would I ever have that kind of relationship?

Oops, I remembered. I am supposed to be focusing on Jack, not fantasizing about someone new. Well, it doesn't count if it's all in my mind, does it? In my mind, I can have what I want, be appreciated, adored and cherished.

With Jack, I didn't know if that could happen, despite my wishing that it would.

WHAT HAD HAPPENED TO MY MARRIAGE?

When Jack and I got married, I was living my dreams. I remember lying next to him in bed and just being happy to be there. I was open with my feelings and made it clear that he was my guy, 'til death do us part. I wanted to do whatever I could to be with him and have a wonderful life. I was free to give him all my love, no holds barred.

But soon after we got married, after we had moved into our little rental cottage on the water, a couple of things happened that put little chinks in my ability to love so freely.

The first was a few weeks after we had moved in together. It was a Saturday morning and Jack was about to rush out of the house. "Where are you going?" I asked, surprised.

"To the Oyster Festival," Jack said. "I am helping my client out with his waffle booth."

"Can I come?" I asked. It sounded like fun.

"No," he said.

"Why not?"

"You need to stay home and deal with yourself," Jack said. "You have to be okay with being by yourself."

He literally left me standing in the driveway. The feeling was familiar, reminding me of my two-year-old incident. I didn't know why I had to stay home. It didn't make any sense and I didn't like it. But for some reason I listened to him like he knew what was best for me. Like I had listened to my parents tell me not to be upset and that I needed to lose weight. I thought they were right. I never questioned them. I had to fix myself.

Jack was now my husband. Marriage was new to me. My mother deferred to my father. He made the decisions. I didn't know not to listen to my husband. I didn't understand why I had to deal with myself, but I thought I had better figure it out.

Years later, when I asked Jack why I couldn't go, he told me that his first wife took four hours to get ready, and he didn't want to have to wait that long. I was not like his first wife. I could have been ready in 5 minutes. But he didn't know that, and he didn't ask.

Looking back, that was what started my old familiar brain pattern of wondering what was wrong with me. *Why did I have to work on being by myself? Why couldn't I come?* Once again, I hated the feeling of being left in the driveway, so I tried to avoid having it happen again by being obedient.

The next incident in our first year of marriage was on Jack's birthday. We had invited his mother and brother over, and I had cooked all day, wanting to make it special for him. I was so excited. When Jack came home from work, he asked me what I was serving.

"Lentil soup and ratatouille," I said proudly.

"That's it? That's what you are serving?"

"Yes."

"You can't serve that. That's not food." He ran out of the house and came back with a loaf of bread and a large piece of salmon. He cooked it on the grill. He placed his food front and center and moved my dishes off to the side.

The humiliation I felt when Jack went out and bought "real food" that night was similar to feeling like the overweight woman on the street. I gave up trusting myself once again, because I had thought what I was serving was delicious, nutritious food.

Instead of telling Jack how hurt I was, I got quiet. Instead of being my real self, I became "good." It was an old pattern. Don't ask for anything, don't be upset, and try not to get criticized. It wasn't fun anymore, but it was safe. And the fun, loving girl that had gotten married, disappeared, and the obedient one replaced her.

16 Throwing Money at the Problem

I tried to feel happy about Jack's renewed enthusiasm about sex, but I wasn't succeeding. "You're not my type," "deal with yourself" and "that's not food" repeated itself in my brain and reignited my hurt and resentment no matter how hard I tried to quiet it down.

I watched as assorted packages started arriving by mail—reading materials, binders, and sex gadgets. Jack was great at throwing money at problems—numerous big black binders filled with diet, exercise, and money-making programs cluttered our small living room.

157

The problem was Jack's follow through. His worst "investment" was paying $14,000 for a master's level investing program. He never made a dime because he quit, saying it wasn't his thing.

Promises, promises. Every time Jack made one, I got my hopes up: the list that was to save our marriage; Sunday night action plans; income goals; budgets; and joint financial decisions. I didn't dare think that this time he might really mean what he said. Why would this time be different? I wondered.

I understood why I wasn't getting excited about his new enthusiasm. I just didn't trust it. So why didn't I just give up on the whole marriage?

Because the anxiety I felt about divorce was more uncomfortable than not having my dreams. The fear of ending up alone was crippling. Deep inside, the simple truth was that I did want the kind of relationship that Jack and I had promised each other in our wedding vows. Was it possible? Was I just fooling myself again?

COULD THIS WORK?

One day I came home from the gym and found Jack on the deck mesmerized by his computer. After a few minutes, he looked up and saw me.

"Come 'ere," he said.

"What? Don't you have work to do? Plus, I have to take a shower," I started heading towards the stairs.

"I think you'll like this."

I groaned. I walked over and looked at the computer screen. There was a diagram of a vagina, and a man was talking. I listened closer. He was describing the different kinds of orgasms that women can have. My mouth dropped open.

"I didn't know there were different kinds," I said, forgetting my annoyance for a few seconds.

"There are three," Jack said, smiling.

"You're kidding." I scrunched up my face. I stared at the video, mouth opening wider.

"Wanna try out what I learned?" he asked.

Do I? I asked myself.

After the last time, I really didn't want to.

Jack was staring at me.

What do I say?

"Um-mm, I have a meeting in 45 minutes. Maybe another time?"

"Okay," he said, smiling, and turned back to his computer screen.

The next day, I was on my way home from an appointment where, when I showed up at the client's office, I was told that he was not in because of an emergency. I was annoyed. I had just talked to him and confirmed the day before.

What a waste of my freaking life.

What should I do with my free hour? I could call Jack and see what he's doing. He's really trying. Maybe my infidelity served a purpose, and this was Jack's wake up call. He's loyal and still there after all these years. I've always wanted him to pay attention to me, and now he is doing that.

I dialed the phone.

"OK, when can I see what you've learned?" I asked Jack.

"What are you doing now?" he asked.

"Well, my meeting just cancelled so I can come home."

"OK, I'll wait."

I let him practice his new techniques and focus on pleasing me. I just laid back and let him do the work. It was pretty good.

Who knows? Maybe this could work.

PART 5

Eyes Opening Some More

1   My New Friend

Instead of once a week, my office started having early morning meetings on Mondays, Wednesday and Fridays. This meant that I had to get to the gym at five a.m. three mornings a week. I noticed new faces. One fifty-ish looking guy caught my eye. He was a regular who was in great shape and very serious about his workout.

One day he got on the elliptical next to me. I wanted to say something, but he just stared straight ahead not looking my way. He started getting off the machine.

I asked, "Where are you going? You just got on."

"To the Stairmaster," he said.

"Why do you switch like that?" I asked.

He stopped long enough to say. "It's not good to do the same thing all the time. I do ten minutes on three different machines."

I've been doing the same thing for years.

I watched him walk away.

His legs were lean but strong. His butt looked like something I wanted to grab and hold onto. His waist was narrow, but he had wide, strong shoulders and a very developed chest. Why was I staring at him? I didn't usually like guys with moustaches. Who knew what kind of hair he had? He always wore a baseball cap.

Another day, I was on the same elliptical and I knew he was in the row behind me on the bicycle. As I got off, I heard him say, "Hey!"

Is he talking to me? My curiosity got the best of me and I turned around.

"I've been enjoying watching your butt," he said.

"You have?" I asked.

"Yup," he said.

I walked off, adding more wiggle because I knew he was watching me. I'm surprised he even noticed me. I practically had to chase him to get him to talk to me last time. Two days later, I was next to him doing my bicep exercises.

"I can't believe I'm getting to the gym this early. If you had told me I'd be doing this two years ago, I wouldn't have believed it."

"I'm used to it," he said. "I've been doing it for years. I especially love coming after early morning sex."

Huh? At four a.m.? Really?

I thought about his comment for days. I couldn't wait to ask him about it.

The next time I saw him, I went straight up to him and said. "You either have a really nice wife or are really good in bed."

He just stared at me with his mouth open.

I laughed. "Last week you told me that you liked to have sex before you came to the gym. For your wife to do that at four a.m., she must either be really nice, or you are really good."

He laughed. "I'm not married," he said.

"Oh, I thought I heard you say you had two kids."

"I do, but I'm divorced."

Then who's he having sex with? I wondered. *And is he available? Why should this even matter to me? I'm supposed to be working on my marriage. Well, at least he's single.*

I still didn't know his name, but I looked forward to seeing him. He wasn't there every day, but if his bag was in its spot, I knew I could find him. One day I hadn't even had time to check for his bag when he came up to me.

"I noticed you stay on the elliptical for a long time. Do you ever do anything else?"

He's single, hot and noticing me again?

I couldn't think of what to say. My body felt warm all of a sudden. "Umm……I do weights three days a week, but otherwise, no," I finally answered.

"You need to mix it up a little if you want to change your body."

He must think I'm fat. Damn it, I thought I was doing so well.

I looked up. He was staring at me.

Oh....

"Are you saying I'm fat? I know I still need to lose…."
"Whoa, no, don't get upset. I didn't say that. Aren't you here to improve your body?"
"I guess," I said, relieved. "I'm glad I asked. I would have obsessed about that comment for weeks."

He smiled. "No need. But try this. It takes 22 minutes and will speed up your metabolism for the rest of the day. Two-minute warm-up. One-minute balls to the wall as hard as you can. Then slow for 30 seconds. Repeat for ten minutes. Then 30 seconds balls to the wall followed by ten seconds for ten minutes."

I repeated what he said to make sure I got it right. "Thanks," I said. "I will. What's your name?"

"Larry."

For the next few weeks, I couldn't wait to thank him, but I didn't see his bag. Finally, I saw it. It was the day after I had had the "go-to guy" conversation with Jack, and I was feeling confused. I found Larry on the stationary bike. His navy baseball cap was pulled over his eyes and he was wearing a light green hoody.

"I did balls to the wall," I said, walking up to him.

"Huh?"

"You know, a minute hard, 30 seconds easy."

"Oh," he said, laughing. "I never called it that. How was it?"

"Hard, but quick. I'm going to change what I'm doing because of what you said. Thank you."

He kept riding the bike.

"Can I talk to you?" I blurted out, getting on the bike next to him. "I don't know you well, but I just feel like I can talk to you. Do you mind?"

"No," he said. "I'm not going anywhere for eight minutes."

"I'm feeling a little mixed up." Larry just looked at me with his eyebrows raised, waiting for me to continue.

"My husband read my private journal and there was stuff in there that was incriminating."

"Why did he go into your stuff? That is so wrong."

"I don't know."

"I would never do that," he said.

Good to know.

"Well, he did, and things have been very intense at home."

"Well, I doubt you did anything that bad."

He finished his bike and walked into the boxing room. I followed him. He started stretching inside the boxing ring. I asked if he minded if I came and stretched with him. I got myself through the ropes of the boxing ring and started imitating his positions.

"It looks like you need to keep talking," he said. "Your secrets are safe with me."

Here goes, I thought.

I told him about my journal, my fantasy life with men, and how Jack was really trying.

"So now he wants to be my go-to guy and have me give up talking to other guys. A part of me feels like I should try to make my marriage work, but the thought of staying married feels like prison with no parole. The gym is the only place where I feel alive and have fun. Does this make sense?" I asked.

"Yes. The gym is the best part of my day, too."

"Really? You feel that way too? You don't think I sound crazy?"

"No. Not at all."

I walked out feeling a calmness I hadn't felt in a while. For the first time in a long time, I felt like someone understood how I was feeling. Larry validated my feelings and it made me feel happy and closer to him. I wanted to talk to him more. I couldn't wait until the next time I saw him.

I finally felt like I had a friend. I wasn't too insecure to go up to Larry. I wanted to talk to him, and I did. I felt like I had conquered another barrier.

2   Lunch with the Girls

Over twenty-five-dollar entrées, my high school friends, Jennifer and Sheri, discussed their home remodeling, vacation plans, and wonderful relationships with their husbands.

I have nothing in common with them, I thought. *What am I doing here? I should be working and making money instead of spending it on this tiny overpriced salad.*

"What's going on?" Sheri asked, interrupting my thoughts.

"Not much," I lied. I ordered another Pinot Gorgio, scrunching my nose as tears popped into my eyes.

"Hey, what's going on?" she asked, putting her hand on my arm.

"My life is so different from yours. I can't imagine remodeling my house or taking a vacation. Jack's philosophy is to spend money whether he has it or not. He lost his main client several years ago and we haven't been making enough to even cover our monthly expenses. Jack uses our home equity loan like a checking account and our debt just keeps going up. I live in a constant state of stress."

They just stared at me. I decided to keep going. I updated them on what had been happening, skipping the part about Claudio. I didn't think that was necessary right now.

"The problem is, I should be happy now that he's paying attention, but I just feel dead." The tears were falling freely at this point.

"Have you ever talked to someone?" Jennifer said, handing me a tissue.

"No."

"I like Jack, but you're not happy. You should talk to someone," Sheri added.

"I don't have the money. Plus, I've tried therapy twice and it was horrible."

"You could find somebody good. I'll get you the name of who I use. Have you ever thought about getting divorced?" Jennifer asked.

"I can't even go there," I said. "I don't want to end up alone."

"You won't. You could find someone great and enjoy your life," Sheri added, touching my arm again. "My husband had a horrible marriage and painful divorce, but then we found each other. We've been incredibly happy for 23 years. If he hadn't been brave enough to leave, he would still be miserable. Like you."

"What if I end up in worse shape because I can't support myself?"

"I'm not worried about you," Jennifer said. "I was always jealous because you were so smart and had such great grades in high school. You'll figure out how to make it work."

I wish it was that easy, I thought. *But if I'm struggling, is Jennifer going to pay my bills? And how could she be jealous of me? I was always jealous of her singing ability. She was Dorothy in 'The Wizard of Oz' in high school and I got put on make-up. That had killed off my dreams of being an actress.*

We continued talking and by the end of lunch, I had the names of both of their therapists.

I was glad I came, I thought. *It felt good to know that they genuinely cared about me and wanted me to be happy. I didn't feel like I was all alone anymore.*

Was the universe trying to tell me something again, like with weight watchers? Two people at my gym had also given me the names of their therapists. That's four names in two weeks. I did a little research and made an appointment.

3   The Therapist

"So, why are you here?" the tiny doctor asked when I showed up for my first appointment.

I told her what was going on. I ended the statement with, "You know what I mean."

"Stop saying 'you know what I mean?' If I don't know, I'll ask you," she said in a nasty tone.

I looked up, stunned. For the rest of the hour I was careful not to use the phrase again. I cried the whole time and finished her box of tissues. The second week I brought my own box. She asked me if I had thought about leaving my marriage.

"I don't know where I would go, or if I could support myself," I said.

"Well, have you figured out how much you would need to live on your own?"

"In my head, but not really."

"Well, why don't you figure it out for next week? That would be a good exercise for you."

"OK, I said, "I feel a little retarded because—"

"Excuse me," she interrupted. "I am on a personal mission to have that word eradicated from our vocabulary. We now say, 'on the spectrum,' and I should know because my grandchild is on the spectrum. Do not say that word again."

Excuse me, I didn't know that was a bad word. We used to always say it growing up. When did that change? I felt like a bad girl who had gotten a spanking. I looked around her cluttered, claustrophobic little room feeling like I wanted to run. One more chance, I thought.

At my third session, we were going over the budget I had put together.

"I don't think I can afford to leave Jack," I sobbed. "I just feel so stuck. I don't want to stay, but I can't leave. I don't know what to do." I blew my nose.

She pulled her glasses down as she looked over the top of my excel spreadsheet. She paused before saying, "I think you should consider medication."

My mouth dropped open. "Are you serious?"

"Yes," she said.

"Why?" I asked.

"So you could be happy."

"I am not here to be happy."

"So you could be less anxious," she added. "I want you to think about it."

Why was she talking to me that way? I didn't come here to be happy. I came so that I could figure out why I was feeling so dead in my marriage. If I can't be myself here without judgment, then what is the point?

I wanted to be able to be okay with what I was feeling, not numb it.

I drove home thinking that she was talking to me like I was a confused, pathetic victim. I didn't blame her for talking to me that way—that's the way I had been acting for a long time.

I didn't used to be that way, I thought. *I had identified that when I did that first transformational weekend course back in 1992. I thought I had gotten rid of being a confused victim.*

Guess not. When things didn't work out as I had planned, I must have gone back to my old default. It was easier to make everything wrong and be a victim than to be responsible for my situation.

I got home and composed an email.

"Thank you so much for your time, but I will not be coming back. These three sessions were exactly what I needed. You did me a big favor by speaking to me like I was a pathetic victim. You have snapped me out of my funk and have given me the greatest gift—remembering who I am. This was perfect. Thank you again."

I hit "Send."

I took a deep breath and closed my eyes. I felt free.

PART 6

Taking Control of My Life

1 Validation – You Don't Think I'm Crazy?

The next day at the gym I walked right up to my new friend Larry.

"Last night this therapist suggested I medicate myself so I could be happy. Can you believe it? I fired her."

I put my bag down and followed him over to the elliptical. I got on the machine next to him.

"I only went three times, but that was enough." I told him what happened.

"All I need is a plan. I can take one action at a time and get myself where I want to go. I am strong. I am woman." I beat my chest like King Kong.

"Back up," he said. "I'm confused. Why did you start going in the first place?"

I outlined the problems in my marriage, ending with the finances and how frustrated I was.

"How could a grown man spend that way?" he asked.

"I don't know. He's a lawyer and very intelligent but has a mental block about finances. It's very strange."

"I don't get it. I couldn't live like that. Suze Orman is my hero. I put away as much money as I can every month and live on a limited budget. I am very frugal," he said with pride.

I looked at him closer. "Really? Me too. When I was single, I lived on a tight budget and monitored every penny. I loved saving as much as I could. I put every raise into savings and never changed my standard of living. I could take vacations when I wanted to. I had a great life then, not like now."

"You must be going nuts," he said. "What are you doing next?"

"Running," I said.

"Let's go," he said.

FINDING THE OLD HILARY AGAIN

We found two treadmills next to each other. I started feeling something different for this man. My legs felt lighter and I noticed I was running much faster than normal.

"So, can you really understand how stressed out I've been?" I asked.

"Absolutely. I can't believe you've lasted this long."

Later when we were stretching, I looked at him closely.

"Can you really get how hard it's been for me to be married to someone who spends like this?"

"Yes," he said.

"And you don't think I'm just crazy and emotional?"

"No," he said. "You make sense."

"Thank you," I said.

I felt like a huge weight had been lifted off me. Not once had Jack understood how stressed out I was over our increasing debt. He had dismissed my concerns every time. Having Larry understand how I felt caused a warm and wonderful feeling to spread over my entire body.

I looked up at the clock. "Gotta go," I yelled. I grabbed my stuff and half ran; half danced to my car. I waved to people as they watched me and smiled at everyone I saw.

Why had I doubted my instincts, I asked myself driving home.

I had not only let Jack rob me of my financial security but also of the most important thing I had—my belief and trust in myself.

I vowed to change things. I was going to take back control of my life and stop being a powerless, confused, insecure victim. All I needed was a plan. I needed to find ways to feel good about myself again. I decided to keep my eyes open.

2 Triathlon

PART 1: JUST AN IDEA

I had always wanted to do a triathlon. I just didn't think I would do it so soon. Every morning, a group of people at the gym exercised together. It always looked like they were having so much fun. I introduced myself to Liz, the ringleader, and she invited me to join them. They did "planks." I didn't even know what that was.

Liz showed me. She leaned on her elbows and pushed her body up. One of the guys put a 45-pound weight on her back. She held herself up for four minutes. It looked easy.

I tried it without the weight. I could barely hold myself up for 15 seconds. "Holy shit," I said. "How do you do that?"

"Keep at it," Liz said. "It's great for your core."

I joined them and became a regular, determined to hold the plank a little longer each time. I loved the new firmness in my core and sides and looked forward to being part of the group every morning.

A few months later, I was talking to one of the "planksters." He told me about a mini triathlon he had done right in town, the week after Labor Day. It consisted of a half-mile swim, ten-mile bike ride, and two-mile run.

I had always wanted to do a triathlon. I started thinking about it. I had been a swimmer growing up and biked and ran for exercise.

Why not? I thought.

I had three months to train.

I started swimming laps in the evening at the town pool, starting with only 20 but adding two every time I went. I forced myself to go two or three times a week. I never wanted to go, but I just followed my plan. Pretty soon, I was doing the half-mile. My goal was to swim double the race distance.

I ran on the treadmill and took spin classes, hating every minute of both the first few times I did them. They were painful, and each minute seemed like hours. I made myself keep to my schedule, doing each one three times a week. After a couple of weeks, I started feeling stronger and more confident.

One day while running I started thinking. *I've proven I could do the distance. I didn't really need to do this. No one even knew I was thinking about it. But it had always been a goal,* I argued with himself. *And I'd come this far. Why stop now?*

Because I was terrified. But I knew myself. If I told people I was doing it, I'd be too embarrassed to wimp out.

I told everyone I knew.

As the triathlon got closer, I had trouble sleeping and worried about all the details I hadn't figured out. One day I was running on the treadmill next to my friend, Larry.

"You're looking good," he said. "You have this triathlon in the bag, don't you?"

"Not quite," I mumbled.

"What do you mean?" he asked. He pressed on the dial to increase his incline.

"I know I can do the distance, but I'm really freaking out about the rest."

"Why?"

"It's a little embarrassing."

"Spill it. After what I've told you about my life, I think I can handle this."

"OK. You asked for it." I leaned over the armrest of his treadmill so I could whisper.

"I can't figure out how to run in a bathing suit. I need a special running bra so I don't bounce too much. TMI?"

"Not at all. Let me think. Okay, I have it. Jump behind a bush after your swim, put the bra over your suit and cover it all with a loose shirt. Sound like a plan?"

"Almost," I said, thinking. *I've never seen any bushes at the beach. I just need to do a little research instead of worrying.*

"What else you got?" he said. He made his speed faster to start running.

I told him how I didn't have a bicycle and I hadn't actually signed up yet.

"Do you think you can do this?" he asked.

"Yes."

"Then pull up your skirt and sign up. Stop being a pussy."

PART 2: COMMITMENT

That night I went online and found the event. There was a $64.00 non-refundable registration fee. Even if it were to be cancelled due to the weather, you didn't get your money back.

I could pray for a hurricane, I thought, *and get out of it gracefully.*

Next, I called my friend, Katherine. She not only agreed to lend me her older bike, but to take me out on training runs in August.

Why did I feel so good? I asked myself. *Because I had identified each obstacle, asked for help, and found solutions. It felt much better than silently worrying, losing sleep and staying stuck.*

Okay. Next, I looked up "triathlon supplies" on Google and found a triathlon store in my town. Amazing. I drove there and told the salesman my dilemma.

He showed me a rack of black, form-fitting, one-piece sleeveless triathlon suits.

"You wear your bra underneath and swim with it on. Then you can bike and run without having to change clothes. Try one," the guy said.

"Great," I said, until I looked at the price tag. "$160 for something I will wear once? I can't rationalize that." I started walking out.

"Wait. Come with me." We went outside to the sidewalk sale rack and flipped through the outfits. "Here's one. It looks like your size. I could give it to you for $60 since it was discontinued."

I took it into the dressing room.

It fit perfectly, but was I down enough in weight to wear something so form-fitting? Plus, it was non-refundable.

"Can you hold this for half an hour?" I asked, throwing the suit on the counter and running to my car. "I need to pick up my daughter."

I brought Haley, then 14, back to the store. "You have to tell me the truth."

"OK, stop talking and just try it on" she said. She was sitting outside the dressing room with arms crossed, scowling.

I came out with my hands over my stomach. She looked me up and down. Then she smiled.

"It's good." She said nodding her head.

"But isn't it too revealing? Is it worth the non-refundable $60?"

"No and yes. It's very cool that you are doing this. Treat yourself, Mom. You deserve it. When do you ever buy something frivolous for yourself?"

"You absolutely should, and you look great," the eavesdropping salesman said. "And, yes, you are worth it." He looked me straight in the eyes as he pointed his finger. "Now go home and sign up. Put your ass on the line."

With triathlon suit in hand, I went home and registered. As I pressed the send button, a chill ran through me. I already felt like a success, and I hadn't even done the race.

PART 3: TRAINING

All through July I made myself swim, run and spin three times a week. There were obstacles like bad weather, work schedules, and kids, but I fit it in. I knew that I needed to stick to my plan. If I didn't, I was afraid that self-doubt would creep into every area of my life. I couldn't afford that.

As August approached, I was having trouble sleeping again. My deadline for swimming in the Long Island Sound, and biking and running outside came and went. On August 8th I was still paralyzed. I confessed my fears to my brother when I visited him in Boston.

"Come on, I'll run with you," he said.

We ran up a hill in his neighborhood.

"How far have we gone?" I asked, panting, struggling to keep up with him.

"About a mile," my brother said. "You better work a little harder. When is this triathlon? You're not in very good shape."

"I have been running," I said. "Running outside is a lot harder than on the treadmill."

"I guess," he said, shaking his head. His mocking grin pissed me off.

Asshole, I thought, sprinting to try to pass him.

He doubled his speed and ran off laughing.

What a jerk, I thought. *I'll show him.*

But at least he got me to run outside. That hurdle was crossed.

FINDING THE OLD HILARY AGAIN

Back home, with only two weeks to go, I still had to get into the Sound.

My mind was screaming but I don't want to.

I dragged myself to the car and started driving to the beach. On the way I called my mother for a distraction from my anxiety.

"Will the lifeguards be there?" she said. "You shouldn't be swimming alone. Call me when you're done. I'll be waiting."

OK, I'll add drowning to my list of things to worry about, I thought.

I walked up to the lifeguard. I was wearing an old one-piece speedo, goggles, and a white swim team bathing cap from the '70s.

"Hi," I said looking up at him in his chair.

He looked at me as if to ask, "You talkin' to me?"

"Um, I'm training for a triathlon, and I'm a little nervous. I've been swimming in a pool and haven't gotten in the real water yet. I have to swim all the way to the end. My mother wanted me to make sure you and the other lifeguards kept your eye on me. Will you?"

How embarrassing, I thought. *I took off my shoes. Just do it.*

I took each painful step over the rocks to the water. I lowered myself into the cold, salty water and started swimming.

This isn't bad, I thought.

I turned my head to breathe. A breaking wave filled my mouth and nose with water. Choking, I decided to quit. I stood up, ready to get out. But then my brother's smirk came to mind.

I will not let him be right.

I started swimming again.

Apart from the saltwater nostril rinse, I made it to the end with no trouble. Instead of walking back, I swam, doing twice what I needed to do in the triathlon.

I got out and ran up to the lifeguard. "I DID IT!!" I yelled, pumping my fists in the air. "I DID IT!" His face was still deadpan, but I swear I saw him wink at me.

The bike was next. We had a disastrous practice run. "I'm quitting," I told Katherine, "I'm too afraid to really get going."

"The seat's too high," she said.

She adjusted the seat. We tried it again. I had visions of hitting a pothole, falling, and ending up under a car. I was so tense that my hands and back cramped.

Was this worth the pain and terror?

I felt like crying.

Instead, I forced myself to follow Katherine. I wasn't going to tell people I was too afraid to ride a bike. I used to ride all over town as a kid.

We kept practicing and I got a little more relaxed each time.

PART 4: RACE DAY

On Race Day, I prayed that the tropical storm that had hit Friday would cause the race to be cancelled. It wasn't. We had been left with a cool, sunny day with rough waves. Great. I could drink more saltwater. I checked into the race in the 50's age group.

My mom, husband and daughter came to watch. When it was my turn, I handed them my outer clothes and waded out with the rest of my peers.

The gun went off and we started swimming.

My swim team training helped, and I finished at the front of the pack. I ran up the beach to my bicycle, struggling to get my running shoes over my sandy feet.

Don't panic, I told myself. *Just keep going.*

I got on my bike and cruised up the hill, feeling fit from my spin classes. My confidence disappeared on the downhill when I couldn't get my bike back into gear. My feet spun around like The Wicked Witch of the West, unable to get traction. The people I had gotten ahead of swimming were passing me no matter how hard I pedaled. The bicycle was obviously broken, but I just kept going, pedaling in the easiest gear without any traction and making my legs go as fast as they could. People kept passing me, but at that point, I just wanted to finish.

I finally reached the changing area and threw down my bike. I tried to start running, but my feet felt like they were encased in cement. Pain shot through me with each forced step I took.

I had run this distance before, what was going on? I wondered. *Oh my God, I had never even thought to do all three together. How was I going to make it? One step at a time,* I thought, *that's all I can do.*

Muttering to myself, I happened to look up.

Was that a mirage?

Was that Liz, my planking buddy?

"Liz," I yelled. "Is that you? What are you doing here?"
"I was out for a run and decided to look for you. How are you doing?" she asked.
"I'm dying. I don't know how I'm going to finish. My legs feel like lead."

"Come on, I'll run you in." She started running with me.

I jabbered nervously, forgetting about the pain. I started running faster. "Liz, you are my angel. I can't believe you were there. Thank you, thank you, thank you!"

We got to the last stretch and I sprinted, giving it my all. I reached the end, breathless, having used up every ounce of energy I had. I looked up. The people in front of me were still running.

"What's going on? That was the end," I gasped.

"I guess it wasn't," Liz said, continuing to run.

"You've got to be kidding. I can't run anymore," I said, gasping.

"Come on, keep going, we're doing this together. You can do it."

"How could that have happened? I can't believe it."

"Stop talking. You're wasting your breath. Follow me and match my stride."

I followed her the rest of the race. I ran through the crowd to the real finish, each step feeling like slow motion, but I made it across the finish line. I turned around to thank Liz and introduce her to my mom, but she had vanished.

That was strange, I thought.

I found out later that "companion runners" do that. They disappear at the end so you can be with the people waiting for you. I grabbed my mom and Haley for a celebratory hug.

"I did it," I yelled, pumping my fists high in the air. "I really did it."

Jack came up to me a few minutes later. "Good job," he said. "Do you mind if I leave now to go to Jesse's hockey game? It's starting in a few minutes." And he left. My mom, Haley, and I stayed for the awards ceremony. I finished somewhere near the middle of my age group

FINDING THE OLD HILARY AGAIN

Not bad for someone with a broken bicycle, I thought.

The euphoria surged through my body for a couple of days. I had pushed myself way beyond what was comfortable and achieved a lifelong dream.

What could I do next? How could I have this amazing feeling again?

3   Jonny and *Success Principles*

PART 1: I USED TO HAVE A DREAM, TOO!!!

"I attribute my success to a book called *Success Principles*," Jonny said. He had been hired by my boss at AFLAC to give a motivational talk about his rise to success. My entire AFLAC office was sitting in our conference room, mesmerized. He had been a single father of three kids searching for a way to support his family, and he was successful at AFLAC.

I wouldn't mind some success, I thought. *I wish I still felt alive like I did after the triathlon. I'm just not a salesperson. I feel dead and barely have enough energy to even lift my arm. How could I convince someone to buy something from me?*

"Since I started reading this book, I have achieved many of my dreams—I have a new wife, a house on a farm with plenty of room, and time with my kids," Jonny said, interrupting my thoughts.

I sat up in my chair.

Dreams? He's living his dreams because of a book? Shit! That stuff sounds familiar. Wait, I used to have dreams, too. I had pictures of them all around my house. I used to be excited and have energy. I used to be like Jonny. What the hell happened to all my dreams?

Then I remembered. Fifteen years before, when Jesse was a few months old, Jack's brother had introduced us to Amway, one of the original multi-level marketing companies. I didn't have any interest in the business until I listened to one of the cassette tapes he had left for us.

The woman on the tape had grown up poor in Appalachia. Newly married with young kids, they could barely survive on her husband's military pay. She went without a coat in winter, too proud to say how cold she was. Her husband surprised her with a coat after making money with Amway. I cried along with her as she described putting on that coat and the lifestyle they now had. I was hooked.

I loved building the Amway business. After being at home with a baby, it was refreshing to get out at night and be part of an adult community. We reached a level of success where I could live one of my dreams—getting paid to travel to speak in front of thousands of Amway distributors across the country. I loved dressing up and being able to tell our story and inspiring others to achieve their dreams.

After about eight years, however, one of our mentors got into trouble and the whole business started unraveling. I desperately clung to the hope that Amway could still solve our financial problems. After two years, however, I could no longer pretend it was still working, and we gave up on the business.

Without Amway, my hope of finding a way to pay off our home equity loan and credit card balances disappeared. My dreams disappeared when I no longer had a way to achieve them. I had literally forgotten about them and become a victim of my circumstances again.

Jonny was still talking. His enthusiasm for life was burning through my resignation. I bit the inside of my mouth, trying to resist the feeling of hope.

At the first break, I followed Jonny into our little office kitchen. I stared at his back as he poured himself coffee.

"Did you ever do the Amway business?" I blurted out as soon as he turned around.

He stared at me as he poured in his cream. "Yes, when I was 20. I was in it for a little while."

"Did you talk about dreams and goals then?"

"Yes, I did."

"I could tell," I said, adding in a whisper. "I did Amway too. I don't tell many people that but back then I had hope for my life. Sitting here, I realized that when the business fell apart and we quit, I gave up on ever having the life I really wanted. Your excitement woke me up. Do you really credit the book with your success?"

"Yes. I do. It's not only working for me, but for my team as well. That can't be an accident."

"I've been struggling a lot lately with how to feel alive again. You came at the perfect time. I can feel myself getting excited already."

"Keep me posted," he said. He touched my arm and looked me in the eyes.

While he finished the rest of his talk, I went online and ordered three copies of Jack Canfield's *Success Principles*. I knew if it was as good as he said, I'd want to start giving it out to my team.

PART 2: RESPONSIBILITY

"If you want to be successful, you have to take 100% responsibility for everything you've experienced in life," Jack Canfield said in his book.

I'm not sure I'm going to like this book, I thought.

I was sitting on my deck reading chapter one. *"Stop blaming others for where you are in life."*

Not blame Jack? But it's his fault, isn't it? If he had shared the same money philosophy as me, we would have a different life. Right?

I swallowed while the nausea crept up my throat.

What if it wasn't all him? What if I had a part in this? It was so much easier to blame him rather than take responsibility for how things turned out. Ugh.

I closed my eyes, feeling the sun through the thick clouds. Resisting the urge to grab the tortilla chips from the kitchen, I stayed still, allowing myself to experience the alternating waves of sadness and disgust.

Why did I blame Jack for my unhappiness? I used to be independent, and I didn't need to rely on anyone for anything. I made my own money and took care of myself. What happened to me?

WHAT HAPPENED TO ME?

I closed my eyes again to try to figure it out. I was doing fine until 1990 when the company I worked for went bankrupt overnight, one Tuesday in February. Almost all the 7,000 Drexel Burnham employees were unemployed as of that Friday. Luckily for me, the controllers' division where I worked was given four weeks to help close the company. My staff found jobs in that time, but I had a harder time since my salary was higher. The headhunters told me that no one was giving interviews to Drexel management because we were overpaid and tainted by the "junk bonds" scandal.

I tried not to listen to their negativity, but I couldn't help it. The timing was terrible. Until a few months before, aside from buying a $300 flute when I was 15, I had never touched my savings. I had accumulated $20,000 from gifts, paychecks, and investments. I felt secure and proud knowing it was there. At 31 years old, I was feeling pretty good.

Earlier that year, I had let my sister convince me to "decorate" my apartment. I didn't mind how it was, but, as always, I thought she was right about how it should look, so I hired her decorator. I was supposed to have $10,000 left, but everything cost twice what I thought it would. My savings were almost gone.

I should have known better, I thought, kicking myself for letting her talk me into it.

I had tried to live into her expectations instead of doing what worked for me.

Plus, being unemployed happened to other people, not me. I was recruited for my first job out of college and then recruited from that job to Drexel.

Since the bankruptcy, my confidence had been replaced by a strange form of amnesia, wiping out my ability to think of a single accomplishment, strength or value I could contribute to a company.

Then on Tuesday of my last week at Drexel with no job in sight, things got even worse. I got a call from a woman who said she had found a Valentine's Day card from me in her boyfriend's pocket.

"Your boyfriend?" I asked. "He told me he had broken up with you."

"Not at all," she said.

We compared notes and realized he had been lying to us both for a long time. He had even given us the exact same gifts for Christmas and Valentine's Day. Did he go in and buy two of everything? I stopped dating him after that, but it now was another part of my life that was disturbing.

On our last Friday, my staff was looking forward to their new jobs. I tried to remain calm and happy for them, but the uncertainty of my own future drowned out everything else.

Trying to remain positive, I met someone that Sunday night to discuss the possibility of starting my own business. The margaritas relaxed me, and I got excited about our discussion. Walking into my building later that night, I reached for my purse and couldn't find it. I ran as fast as I could back to the restaurant, but it was nowhere to be found. All of my identification, credit cards and keys were gone.

Too late to find a locksmith, my doorman drilled a hole in my door to let me in. I spent the night staring at the lockless door, knowing that whoever stole my purse, also had my address and keys.

The next morning, exhausted, I found a token in a jacket pocket and headed up to midtown to get a new bank card.

"I'll need to see your ID," the bank woman said.

"But I don't have it. It was stolen."

"Well, I'm very sorry," she said, not seeming to be sorry at all.

"You can't be serious," I said. "I've been a customer here for six years."

"I'm sorry. Those are the rules." She was looking at my accounts on the computer screen. "Oh, and it looks like your accounts are wiped out—even your line of credit."

"What?" I asked, bursting into tears. She pointed at the screen. I couldn't see it, but it didn't matter. I was beyond being able to hold it together. Sniffling, I asked, "What am I going to do? I don't even have a token to get home."

For a long moment, she looked at me. Her demeanor finally softened as she opened her drawer, took out a token and handed it to me. "Take this. Try American Express. There's an office on Wall Street."

FINDING THE OLD HILARY AGAIN

"Thank you," I said. I grabbed a handful of tissues from the box on her desk. I left the building and heading to the six train.

The subway was packed, but I found a seat. I sat down and put my head in my hands. My chest felt like it would explode, and I had trouble breathing. My head was filled with visions of me homeless, lying on a piece of cardboard on the street. I shuddered at the image of my face, red, bloated and covered with filthy, stringy hair. I shook my head, trying to clear the picture from my brain.

Please God, I thought. *I can't handle one more thing going wrong. I am asking for help. I don't know what to do anymore.*

I took a deep breath gasping at the stench of the homeless man sitting next to me. No wonder the seat had been free. I barely breathed until we got to my stop.

After my prayer, everything seemed to turn around.

Feeling desperate, I got to the American Express office and without any problems, they issued me a new gold card. I started to breathe and went back to the bank. The woman who had told me my accounts were emptied looked at them again. "Oh! They're fine," she said. "I guess I made a mistake."

I was too exhausted to tell her about the additional stress she had caused me. I went home. There was a message from a stranger telling me he had found my purse. I went back uptown and met him on the steps of St. Patrick's Cathedral, and he returned it to me. The thief had taken only the cash and thrown the purse into the dirty linens. This nice man had found it.

I went back downtown to my apartment. There was a phone message saying I could stay and work at Drexel for another three months, as if I had never been let go. I would get time-and-a-half, and if I stayed the whole three months, I would get another half pay, resulting in twice as much as I had been making. I ended up finding a job the day before the three months was up. In the end, I was better off than I had been before!

I believe God answered my prayers that day. I was never actually unemployed, but the emotional scars had still not healed. The bold, outspoken Wharton grad who had never doubted herself had disappeared. She was replaced by someone who was dependent on others.

I held onto a job I hated for the next five years because I was afraid to take a risk and leave. The terror of my experience had been so painful that it became easier to rely on others and avoid having to experience that anxiety again. Once married, I hid behind Jack's earning ability and never addressed my lost confidence.

Looking back, I see that my fears of being homeless were completely irrational. I could have sold my apartment or gotten help from my parents, who were only an hour away. There were plenty of friends and family who would never let me sleep on the streets.

But at that time, I was stuck in my own terror-filled mind and never thought of asking for help. I was paralyzed by my stable, secure world being turned upside down. My unknown and unsafe future locked me in my own mind—never thinking of letting anyone find out how desperate I felt.

I knew I was scared after Drexel went bankrupt, but I didn't know I had lost so much of who I was.

Was it possible for me to feel capable of supporting myself again?

Could I become that independent, confident, fearless Hilary again?

I decided to keep reading….

FINDING THE OLD HILARY AGAIN

PART 3: MORE ABOUT RESPONSIBILITY

"If you want to have the life of your dreams… it means giving up all your excuses, all your victim stories, all the reasons why you can't and why you haven't up until now, and all your blaming of outside circumstances. You have to give them up forever," the book said.

I sat on my deck reading *The Success Principles* the next day. The clouds were out so I went inside to put on my favorite maroon fleece hoody.

"You've sat passively by and let your life happen to you," the book went on.

I didn't know I had, I thought.

I massaged my back where it had started hurting. Financially I had done everything I could think of—created budgets, hid the credit cards, sought out financial planners, and kept detailed track of everything we spent for years. Nothing had made a difference.

I looked at the book. *"You pretend not to see and not to know because it is easier, more convenient and less uncomfortable, avoids confrontation, keeps the peace, and protects you from having to take risks."*

That's what I've been doing, I thought, feeling disgusted. *When nothing I did worked, it was easier to start blaming Jack instead of continuing to look for solutions.*

And our relationship? I wondered, tears threatening. *Did I quit on that, too? No, I couldn't have*, I thought, rubbing my throbbing head.

I read all the relationship books, attended marriage seminars, and had meaningful conversations with Jack. Every time he didn't keep his wonderful heartfelt promises, the cycle of shock, disappointment, self-doubt, despair and despondency repeated itself. Having no reference point for marriage, I blamed myself for not being the kind of woman a man could be attracted to. Then I pretended everything was ok.

I'm afraid to hope. I don't want to be disappointed again.

I closed my eyes as the tightness in my chest spread down to my stomach. The sadness of the past seemed overwhelming.

I opened my eyes and happened to glance at the book. "If you focus on what you don't want, that's what you'll get," it said.

Oh, I guess that's what I'm doing, I thought.

I looked ahead at the next chapters.

"*See What You Want, Get What You See,*" and "*Experience Your Fear and Take Action Anyway.*" This book was talking to me. The sun popped out of the clouds.

Thank you, God. I'm assuming that was a sign. You're right. I have nothing to lose.

PART 4: PURPOSE

The next day I brought *Success Principles* out onto the deck again.

I opened chapter two: *Be Clear Why You're Here.* "Each one of us is born with a life purpose," it said. I used to have a purpose. I was excited about it back then. I did the exercise in the book, wondering if it would come out the same. It did. I smiled, remembering the day 20 years before when I had figured it out.

I was still single, living in New York City. I was in one of my transformational programs and our assignment was to discover our "possibility" or purpose.

I thought back to when I was really happy as a kid. I used to pretend that I was special. When I talked to Paul McCartney's picture, I imagined that he loved me and accepted me just as I was. I could say anything to him and wasn't criticized or judged.

I had always wanted to find a real person like that. I could be myself with him. We would relax and enjoy and empower each other to be the best people we could be. We would be able to achieve whatever we were passionate about. I started getting excited.

I wanted everyone to be able to live their dreams—the ones that they had when they were little. Maybe they got resigned or cynical about them and gave up. What if everyone could have passionate lives doing what they love? I started bouncing in my chair, getting clear about what I would say.

When it was my turn to declare my possibility, I confidently climbed onto the platform, faced the audience and boldly stated, "I am the possibility of inspiring people to live the lives they've always dreamed of."

There was a moment of silence. I waited.

"Excellent," the instructors said. "We really get it. You pass."

I felt great. Next up was Alison, a shy, soft-spoken girl. She mumbled something. She was looking down, so I couldn't hear what it was. I felt a little sorry for her.

"No pass, Alison," the judges said. "Sorry. You," they pointed at me, "go work with Alison. She is struggling." I took Alison out of the room, proud that they thought I could help her. She was confused and couldn't even tell me what she was interested in.

"Well, when are you the happiest? When do you not notice the clock and get lost in what you are doing?"

She thought for a few minutes. "Anything with nature," she said, her face lighting up.

"What about nature? Which part do you love?" I kept asking her questions until she could state her purpose clearly.

She went back and climbed onto the platform. She looked the instructors right in the eyes, and loudly proclaimed "I am the possibility of creating a world where nature thrives as God meant it to."

Beth, the instructor, looked at me and said, "You are an excellent coach." I was thrilled, not just from the praise, but because it felt so good to help Alison get clear about her purpose. I felt alive.

After that, whenever I got an opportunity to volunteer as a coach, I offered my services. I loved it so much I started practicing on my friends, charging them $25 a month. Each month I increased my fees and within a year, I was charging $500 a month. I helped one friend raise $1 million for his business. Another woman started a business. Three people were able to distinguish their destructive relationship patterns and create new ones. All three ended up getting married.

How could someone who wasn't in a relationship herself coach these people? I think I was good because I didn't judge. And since I had made all the dating mistakes myself, theirs were easy to see. Those of us who struggle sometimes make the best teachers. The coach isn't always the best player but someone who can take an athlete to a level they can't reach by themselves.

When I got married, I quit my job to start a full-time coaching business in Connecticut. It started out great. My clients came from my warm network who understood the value of a coach. Unfortunately, my success was short lived.

Every mistake I made ended up costing me a client. In Connecticut, it was much more difficult to find clients. The people there weren't familiar with the role of a coach. Then, when I had my son, it was easier to focus on being a mother. I didn't replace my clients as they achieved their goals. I became a "stay at home" mom, and in the process, became financially dependent on Jack. It didn't seem like a problem since he was doing well as a lawyer back then.

But now, sitting out on my deck, I wondered if I could ever be independent again.

I better read some more, I thought. I was getting depressed.

"When you are living true to your purpose, you experience joy and passion."

FINDING THE OLD HILARY AGAIN

Maybe that was true. When I was coaching, I was helping people discover their dreams, and I felt alive. I helped them develop goals and encouraged them when they wanted to quit. I was passionate, just like Jonny was when he spoke to us.

Could I ever get back the confidence, success and excitement that I used to have?

I shifted positions on my deck chair and scratched my head. A few years before, the kids no longer needed me as much, and I figured I would try to start my coaching business again. I was shocked that the coaching industry had grown. Twenty years before, it was a new concept and my coaching was a novelty. Now, coaches were everywhere trying to get clients. I tried not to be discouraged and spent $3,000 on designing beautiful postcards and business cards. When I didn't get any clients, I decided to cut my losses and look for a business that could make money.

The twelfth business we looked at was AFLAC. I liked the people, and AFLAC did the marketing for us. When money started coming into our account instead of out, we decided to pursue it instead of going for the 13th business idea.

Could I become independent again? Could I bring my purpose to AFLAC and feel confident and excited again?

I knew I was inspiring people with my weight loss, work outs, and how my body was changing. I looked up at the clouds, distracted by the shapes swirling in the sky.

What else could I do to inspire people? How could I become passionate and confident enough to be independent?

I closed my eyes, taking a deep breath of the salt air. I got up to make a fresh pot of coffee.

Taking a sip, I decided to do what I had done at my last job after identifying my purpose. I acknowledged people and found out what they loved to do. Since I was a manager, I took an interest in my associates and helped them to develop goals. I coached them to achieve more success than they had been having.

Even though I wasn't being specifically paid to coach, it ended up being fun and resulted in my group doing much better than they had been. Success was way more fun than failure. I got excited about what I was doing, and that excitement was contagious. I silently thanked Jonny for inspiring me to dust off my dreams again.

4 You're Eating Too Much

It was October 2012, shortly after I started reading *The Success Principles*.
"I don't know what I'm doing wrong," I whined. I got off the scale. "I track, I eat according to plan, I exercise. I've been stuck for over a year. Not only am I not losing, but I'm gaining. I am so frustrated!" Every week I vented to Lynn, our Weight Watchers weigh-in lady.

What could she possibly say? I thought to myself. *It's not her problem.*

"Why don't you talk to Joyce, our new leader?" she asked.

"I did. She told me to eat more, the last one said to eat less, and the other one said drink more water. Whatever I try, it doesn't work."

The meeting was about to start, and we all went in. I had been on Weight Watchers for over two years and was down 25 pounds. I took a seat in the back of the room.

"This week I lost 3 pounds," a new girl said, jumping up and down.

I was sitting with my arms crossed, the resentment building in my neck and back. "Whoop-dee-do" I said under my breath. "I hate her and her and her."

Each woman shared her successes and triumphs. I tried to rub out the knots in my lower back, realizing I was slouched over in pain. I rummaged through my purse and took out two ibuprofen and a bottle of water.

I sat in my chair reviewing the previous few months, trying to figure out what I was doing wrong. I had written down my goals and put them in my phone. I had finished *Success Principles*.

Why was I gaining weight instead of losing?

I wanted to scream.

After the meeting, I went up to Debbie, the district manager for weight watchers who happened to be visiting our meeting that day. I had never spoken to her before.

"Debbie, I don't know what to do. I've been stuck for over a year. Some people tell me to eat more, some people tell me to—."

"You're eating too much," she said interrupting me.

"What?" I said, ignoring her rude tone.

"You're eating too much. It's simple. When you eat less, you lose weight. End of story," and she turned around to talk to the next person.

How dare you? I thought.

I was about to grab her and turn her around so I could tell her what I thought of her. Instead, I clenched my teeth and walked out of the church where the meeting was held.

Fuck her, I thought, putting my sunglasses on.

I crossed the street and unlocked my car.

What if she's right?

I got in the car. I watched the children on the church playground without really seeing them.

Was I really being honest with myself about how much I was eating? Was I really measuring my portions? Did food like margaritas and nachos have more points than I was counting? Was I kidding myself?

I started driving. It reminded me of another time when I couldn't figure out what I was doing wrong. Twenty years before, I was playing in a tennis tournament out in the Hamptons. I had beaten my opponent 6-1 in the first set. We were now in the second, and she was ahead, 4-1. I was panicking. I looked around. My housemate happened to be playing on the court next to me.

"What am I doing wrong?" I asked as softly as I could. "I was winning before."

"You stopped running when you started winning," she said, as if it was obvious.

"Oh," I said. "I had no idea. Thanks."

For the rest of the match, I ran ahead of the ball, got into position, and strategically placed the ball. I beat her 6-4, went to the finals, and won the club tournament that summer. I learned a valuable lesson and won for the first time instead of choking in the finals. I kept my eye on what I needed to do, instead of on the score.

I could see that this was a pattern for my life. In sales when I thought I had a client sold, I stopped listening and blew the sale. In tennis and squash, I would start out winning and end up losing. It was happening with my weight loss. I had gotten close to my goal weight a year before. Since then, the scale was creeping back.

I got home and took out my *Success Principles* book. I started re-reading the goal setting chapters. I looked at my goal of weighing 146, the top of the maintenance range for my height—August 30, Sept 30, Oct 31 were all crossed off. I was tired of resetting the dates. What was I missing?

FINDING THE OLD HILARY AGAIN

It was staring me in the face. *"Decide what you want," "Believe It's Possible"* and *"Believe in Yourself"* were chapters I had skimmed and missed my first time through. I really didn't think my goal weight was possible, I realized. I knew my friend Jennifer had gotten to her goal weight, but I honestly didn't think Fat Hilary could ever be thin enough not to have to lose more weight. It was a concept I couldn't comprehend. I had always had to lose weight. My whole life.

I looked at the book again. I had to ACT AS IF I had already reached my goal, using the emotions involved to lock it into my subconscious mind. The subconscious would then go to work bridging the gap between reality and the visualization. Could I suspend my disbelief and pretend-try this? It didn't really seem like it could work.

So many times before when I hadn't reached my goals, I had just given up and set them aside. What if I just tried to do what the book said? Was there anything to lose?

Still sitting on my deck, I closed my eyes. I pictured myself proudly seeing 146 on the scale. In slow motion, I clench my fists raising them above my head in a Victory V. I jump up and down and start doing the happy dance. I looked back at the book and changed what was written on my goal card imitating the example in the book.

"I am joyously celebrating becoming a lifetime member of weight watchers on Jan. 1, 2013. I love knowing my lifetime membership is free forever." I made several copies and put them where I would see them every day.

The next morning, after visualizing my victory dance, instead of just estimating what I was eating, I started measuring again. I made sure that I was within my points for each day. I didn't know if it would make a difference, but I was feeling good about having a plan.

"Lynn, it's working," I whispered a couple of weeks later, stepping off the scale. "I am visualizing my success every morning. I'm measuring my food again and staying within my points. The weight is finally coming off. Hallelujah."

"Keep it up," she said, gently squeezing my shoulder.

"Hey, will you take a picture of me doing my victory dance?"

"Absolutely. Go up with Joyce. I'll take it." I went up and raised my arms above my head, fists clenched, dancing with Joyce. We spun each other around, just like I did every morning in my mind. The weight kept coming off.

Six weeks later, the day I was to hit my goal weight, I was too nervous to wait another day for my once-a-week Westport meeting. I went to the Norwalk center and got on the scale. It read 146. Not 0.2 above or below. I couldn't believe it. I just stared. Then reality hit, and I raised my arms in the air and started dancing.

"What am I missing?" the weigh-in lady said.

"I'm in maintenance range for the first time in my life. I never thought I would actually do this," I said, emotion almost preventing me from speaking. I savored the moment, thinking of my lifelong weight struggle. I never felt like I was thin enough, no matter how much I weighed.

"Congratulations," the woman said. She took out a pamphlet. "Hold this for six weeks and you become Lifetime. Your membership will be free."

"Yes," I said, snapping out of it. I pumped my arms some more, still jumping up and down. I was too excited to put my shoes on yet.

"Oh my god," I realized. "I have to hold this for six weeks? This is over Christmas and New Year's. Holy hell. Wish me luck."

"Good luck," she said.

5   Revising My Goals

About a month after I started reading *The Success Principles*, I was on the bike at the gym. Trying to heed Jonny's advice, I took out my *Success Principles* and forced myself to read a chapter. After that, I reached into my bag hanging from the handle of the bike and pulled out my index cards. I looked at my goals.

I wasn't getting the goal thing. I was still confused about the difference between goals, affirmations, and visualizations. I reviewed those chapters again, trying to get what I was missing. I took out some blank index cards from my bag and started writing new goals while I leaned on the console of the bike.

"I am enjoying the thrill of seeing my first book on *The New York Times Book Review*. I love knowing it is a best-seller and inspiring millions around the world."

"I am so happy to be appearing on today's Oprah."

This was kind of fun.

I kept writing. Goals for my weight, relationships, and the women's empowerment group that I wanted to start. I closed my eyes to visualize how I would feel if each goal were accomplished. It started feeling like I had achieved them.

Amazing, I thought.

Maybe I did need the emotions attached to them to make them real. It didn't matter if I believed it, I just had to act like they were already accomplished.

I kept pedaling. Was I asking for too much? If people saw my list, would they laugh? Oh, why was I worrying about what other people thought. Where had that gotten me my whole life? I took out a new card and took a deep breath.

I trust the process of life. I breathe deeply and peacefully and trust and enjoy the moment.

I realized that for the past few years, I had been focusing on what I didn't want and what I was afraid of. That had just gotten me more of the same. How was I going to remember to visualize what I wanted instead? And visualize it already happening? I guess that's what the cards were for. To remind me. I put them in my bag where I would see them every day. According to the book, my subconscious would figure out how to accomplish my goals. I didn't need to worry about the "how", which took a lot of pressure off.

I added one more card, *I am happy with myself and knowing God loves me and blesses me and my purpose. I am feeling confident, loved, peaceful and secure in His Love.*

"Ok, I thought. Enough for today." I put away the last card and took out one of my happy-ending books. Now I could escape into their world, my reward for doing my work. I pedaled harder, took a deep breath and smiled.

6 Women's Empowerment Group

I read the last chapter of *Success Principles*. Jack Canfield said, "*If you teach the principles to others, they will stay alive for you.*" I started getting a nervous feeling in my chest. I kept reading. "*Just download the guidelines from the success principles website and start a group.*"

I had always wanted to start a women's empowerment group. I loved the idea of women supporting each other in accomplishing the goals they were afraid to take on alone.

Before I could chicken out, I went to the website and downloaded the document. I called my friends and asked them if they wanted to be a part of my women's group.

We met in the "Jonny" conference room at my AFLAC office. I told them what had been happening since I started reading the *Success Principles* and passed out index cards for them to write down their own goals. The women introduced themselves, giving some background and what they wanted to accomplish through the group.

When it was my turn, I was ready to discuss my writing and work goals, but when I opened my mouth, I was too choked up to speak. I stood by my chair, trying to compose myself. My hand started shaking as I walked over to the white board on my office wall. I drew a teeny little scared mouse in the lower left corner of the board. "This is who I've become since I got married," I said.

Then I drew a large stick figure holding up the world that covered most of the rest of the large board. "This is who I was before I got married, and who I've been trying to uncover for the last couple of years. I feel like this when I'm not around Jack. Like I could accomplish anything."

The other women just looked at me. "We had no idea," they said. "We like Jack, but if your marriage isn't working, you need to do something. We will support you in whatever you decide." We scheduled another time to meet and named ourselves WET, for Women's Empowerment Team.

Cleaning up the office that night, I realized it was perfect timing for all of us. We each had a different set of challenges. We got to listen, support and pray for each other. The bonding, love, empowerment and gratitude was overwhelming.

I stopped cleaning and looked at the two pictures of me on the board. I blinked a few times. I must have imagined the stick figure holding up the world winking at me.

7 Cracking a Piece of the Shell

It was late November 2012, a few months after my triathlon. I had started going to the gym at 4:30 every morning in the hopes of seeing Larry. I didn't know his schedule, so never knew when he would be there.

It was hard to believe that someone who loved sleeping late as a child was willing to get up at four a.m. for anything. The chance to see Larry was highly motivating. I had developed an emotional attachment to him and lived for the days I would see him. Being able to just go up to him and talk without being worried about bothering him was something I had never thought I could have.

We had gotten close. We confided in and encouraged each other. If I was upset one day, I got to talk. Some days it was Larry who needed to talk. I loved having someone I could share my feelings and fears with, someone who understood and validated me. It felt like magic.

I knew I had feelings for him, but all I had gotten back were subtle comments that confused me. I had no idea if he felt anything for me. I thought about a conversation we had had a month before. We were stretching on the grassy area. He had looked at me as if he had just thought of something.

"I really like talking to you. You make me think. I am very comfortable telling you things that I don't tell anybody else." He paused and switched into a different stretch. Keeping his head down, he said, "Maybe we can have coffee someday and just talk when we are not at the gym and not rushing."

When? Today? Now? Keep going, I thought.

But he didn't say anything else. "Okay," I said eagerly. I wanted to ask him when, but I resisted.

FINDING THE OLD HILARY AGAIN

When he didn't mention it again for a month, I could hardly stand it. I tried to figure out a way to bring it up. He knew I sold AFLAC, and one day he mentioned that he might look at getting an AFLAC policy for himself.

That's it, I thought.

I kept after him to set up a time to have coffee. Since it was for business, I didn't feel like I was chasing him even though I felt a little pathetic in my level of desperation. I didn't really care. I just wanted to see him outside the gym and push the relationship a little further.

It took a few more weeks, but he finally agreed to set a date. I went to Ann Taylor and bought a couple of new dresses, rationalizing that I needed them for work.

We agreed to meet at Dunkin' Donuts near my office at three o'clock one afternoon. I wore my new blue dress that brought out my eyes and showed off my figure the best.

I could barely get through the day. I was so nervous; I couldn't even eat—extremely rare for me.

I walked in and looked around. I stared. I almost didn't recognize him without his standard baseball hat. He was sitting at a table wearing his bulky plaid flannel jacket and jeans. His beard had grown in since the morning at the gym. His hair was gray and fluffy. His face looked different from the morning, young kid look under the baseball hat.

"I hate you," he said.

"Huh?" I said.

"Oh nothing, that's just something I say," he said.

What did that mean?

Confused, my heart still went crazy.

What was it about this guy that affected me so physically?

I blabbered something about getting my coffee. I put my computer on the table and walked to the counter wondering if he was watching me. I couldn't believe I was finally seeing him outside of the gym. I couldn't think clearly.

I came back with my coffee and opened my computer, ready to give him the AFLAC rates. He didn't seem that interested, but I gave him some numbers anyway. He told me he'd think about it.

I was ready to discuss our relationship. I had practiced it in my mind hundreds of times. I was going to ask him if he felt the same way I did. I needed to know. But I just stared at him, tongue-tied.

He leaned back in his chair and smiled. "So, tell me about your husband," he said.

What? Seriously? Why do you want to talk about him?

I wanted to scream. But instead, I said, "Jack used to be a lawyer but wasn't interested in doing that anymore. He ......"

"He went to law school? Wow. Where did he go to college?"

"Brown University and Fordham Law."

"He's my hero. I wish I had studied harder when I was younger. I played and now I am paying for it. I try to teach that to my kids, but they don't really listen to me. I wish I could have been like Jack."

This was not going the way I had pictured. He peppered me with questions about Jack for the next 20 minutes. I was silently seething. I let him go on and on until I couldn't stand it anymore.

"But what's so great about a guy who can't pay his bills?" I finally blurted out. "Why does that make him a hero? Why do you think that is so admirable?"

"How could he not? I pay all my bills ahead of time," Larry said. "I save over $2,000 a month. I work 80 hours a week. I'm blue collar but I have money set aside, retirement planned for, and I am paying my mortgage twice a month to reduce the debt faster."

I started feeling sick. He took out a pen and started writing figures on a napkin. He had money in his pension, in savings, college put away for the kids, and no debt.

I couldn't breathe. "That's what I thought I would have after 16 years of marriage," I said. "But instead, here are two freaking Ivy League graduates who can't pay their bills. I feel lucky if I can cover Jack's negative balances every day. You are acting like he is something special, but I think what you have done is way more admirable."

Larry shook his head. "But Jack has a graduate degree. Surely he can go get another law job and make a lot of money."

"He could, but he won't. He's not like you. He doesn't even think about saving money and we often need to refinance the house to pay the bills and taxes. Why do you think he is so much better than you?"

He didn't answer. He stood up. "I gotta go," he said and walked me to my car.

I got in my car and just wanted to cry. The pit in my stomach got worse. What a freaking disappointment.

I was too upset to go back to work. I drove over to the local beach and stared at the water. A seagull made a deposit on my windshield.

Great. Just what I needed.

I had wasted all these years by not saving money like I knew I should have. Larry was saving. He was paying off his mortgage instead of refinancing like Jack. We had more debt now than when we bought the house. Larry was making two payments to reduce his debt. My head hurt, and I just wanted to go to sleep. I closed my eyes and felt the warm sun coming through the windshield. I must have fallen asleep.

I opened my eyes, confused about where I was.

Damn it. I still didn't know if Larry felt anything for me. I guess we were destined to just be friends.

I was annoyed but knew there was nothing I could do about it that day.

I drove back to my office. The financial conversation haunted me. I couldn't do anything about my relationship, but I could do something about my finances. I had heard other women talk about their secret bank accounts that their husbands didn't know about. They socked away money whenever they could. They didn't seem to feel bad about it, instead sounded giddy. And they had money if they needed it.

So why did I feel bad just thinking about it?

I had never been secretive with Jack about money. I wanted to be honest, but where had that gotten me?

A few days later, I decided to take action. On November 28, 2012, I drove to TD Bank. Before I got out of the car, I looked around to make sure Jack's car was not in the area. I felt sneaky. I walked in and whispered to the lady at the counter.

"Where can I open an account?"

"Over here. Come right over to this chair and have a seat."

"Nothing can be sent to my house," I said. "Is that possible?"

"Absolutely," she said. I had never met her, but she made me feel like we were close friends.

"Ok, let's do it," I said.

I filled out the forms and gave her an AFLAC bonus check to deposit. Driving home that day I felt guilt mixed with elation. I had my own account with $5,539 in it that Jack didn't know about. I was finally taking my finances into my own hands. I smiled thinking about how I would make deposits into it whenever I could. Increasing my savings made me feel like I was making progress in life.

I was surprised that I was crying again. It felt like I was breaking through some kind of physical barrier that had covered me during my marriage. I had thought I was being a "good wife" by deferring to Jack's way of doing things. Only now did I realize that it had robbed me of my power. I had sacrificed my own sense of security and safety in the process.

Even though I was disappointed that my conversation with Larry hadn't gone in a romantic direction, talking about his finances had done something more valuable. It had cracked open another part of the shell that had grown over me during my marriage, and I felt just a little more in control of my own life.

8 The One Area not Progressing

I was reading my relationship goals while on the elliptical one morning. Why did I just get depressed? I asked myself, looking at the card. Because I knew deep inside that staying with Jack meant I'd never have the relationship I had always dreamed of. I couldn't see myself being passionate, self-expressed, financially free and loving my life with him. It seemed like I had to either give up on my dreams and stay married or go after them and leave him.

Both options scare me, I thought as I exercised.

I saw Larry come into the cardio area and get onto the bike. We had become good friends in the last few months, and I was very attracted to him. My crush had gotten much worse. I still lived for the mornings when he was there.

How does he feel? *I would ask myself.*

Coming back to the present, I got off my machine and got on the bike next to him. "Can I talk to you?" I asked.

"Sure, what's up?" he responded, pedaling fast and adjusting the brim of his baseball cap.

"I just need to distract myself from my thoughts. I'm getting myself depressed."

"Why? What's going on?"

"The only place I'm happy is in my little fantasies in my mind. I can have whatever I want there," I said.

"Me too. I always have the best times in my fantasies," he said.

"Tell me one."

"Let's see, we fly down to one of the islands. Which one do you want to go to?"

He said we. I think he's talking about me and him. Hallelujah.

I was smiling widely as we walked over to the stretching area. "Let's see, let's go to St. Maarten. I've never been there."

"Ok, on the plane we snuggle together under the blanket and have a nice nap. When we arrive, we spend some time on the beach and take a swim. We go back to the hotel, shower, and you put on a yellow sundress. We go out to dinner. Afterwards we slow dance together and end up making out in the hallway with you pressed up against the wall."

Sounds great to me, I thought, desire having replaced my depression.

"You should be a writer. You are really good at this," I said, smiling. I turned over on my stomach. "You could help me write book two. We could travel first class around the world, and you could help me write about our sexual adventures together. Would you want to?"

"Sure," he said absently. "But this is my fantasy, not yours. Let me finish."

"Oh, ok," I said, trying not to be insulted that he didn't jump at the chance to be in my fantasy. "Then what?"

"We take a nice romantic walk on the beach, holding hands and looking at the moon reflecting on the water. Then, I walk you to your room and say good night."

"What?" I said.

"I put you in your room, and I go to mine," he said.

"After all that, we don't share a room?" I couldn't help asking. "Forget it. I couldn't take it. What's the point?"

He just laughed. I stared at him, but he didn't say anything. "Seriously?" I asked.

"Well, I don't really know you well enough to share a room," he said.

Since when? I asked myself. *I felt like I knew him intimately. Was he kidding, or did he not feel what I was feeling? I think I'm in love with this man.*

I loved the excitement that ran through me when I was with him. I loved talking to him. I loved that we shared the same philosophy about money. I loved his passion at the gym, how hard he worked and how financially responsible he was for his kids.

Was I attracted to him just because I wasn't getting that from Jack? Did Larry seem better because I was comparing him to Jack? Was that a fair thing to do?

I thought about it for a few minutes. All I knew was that I felt happy and good about myself when I was with Larry. At home, I felt insecure and misunderstood.

Jack said it was wrong to get emotionally attached to someone who wasn't my husband. Well, it was too late. I already was. And, whether I liked it or not, my body responded to Larry whether I wanted it to or not.

The big question was did Larry feel what I felt? Was he happy just being friends? I really wanted to know. But it wasn't the right time or place to ask. I was going to find out, I just didn't know how.

9 Do You Have Time?

It was Thursday at 5:00 AM, the day before the 2012 New Year's holiday weekend. I was on the elliptical at the gym, watching Larry do his weight routine. My heart was beating faster than it ever had before.

How was I going to do this? I wondered.

My goal was to finish my book by December 31. I really wanted a happy ending—Larry and I walk off into the sunset, profess our undying love for each other and live happily ever after. It may sound crazy, but at that time it was all I could think about.

I had to force this to happen fast since I was going to Vermont with the kids and Jack the next day to spend New Year's with his friends. I felt desperate to find out how Larry felt about me.

When I wrote my relationship goals, I finally admitted to myself that I had based them on the relationship I could see having with Larry. Even though I didn't know him well when I wrote them, I loved the way he talked about us going away together. I had always dreamed of being with a romantic, loving, passionate man who was loyal and crazy about me.

I saw him go to the stretching area and followed him. I asked if I could join him.

"Of course," he said. I got down on a mat on the floor next to him, the fake green grass tickling my legs where they were hanging off the matt. I told him that Jack wanted to go to Vermont for the weekend to visit with some friends, but that I wasn't really thrilled about going.

"I think it would be good for the kids," I said. "But I'd rather stay home."

We switched stretches. My heart was racing.

How was I going to ask him? What could I say?

"Will you have time after work to have coffee? I want to talk to you about something," I said with my head hanging down.

He thought a minute. "No, I don't have time, but why don't you tell me now, I have a few minutes."

I just looked at him. I couldn't formulate the words. I wasn't ready.

How could I ask him? What if he didn't feel the same?

"I'm too embarrassed to say it here," I finally said.

He scrunched up his face, looking at me. He made a few guesses about what it could be, but I just said no, that's not it. It was hard for me to breathe.

How would I know? How could I get a happy ending by Monday? What was I going to do? How would I know how to end this book?

The disappointment and panic filled my tense muscles even though I was trying to stretch them out. I felt the tears building so I kept my head down so he couldn't see.

"Don't worry about it," I said, pretending, as usual, that I was fine. I wanted to add, *And I have my answer if you don't have time for me*, but I didn't. I didn't want to let him know I cared. We walked out making small talk. Inside, I felt a mixture of panic and disappointment. I didn't know whether to grab him and not let him leave me, or just go hide in the corner and curl up in a ball.

The next morning, I had time to come to the gym before we left. I purposely stayed away from Larry; afraid he would ask me what I wanted to talk to him about. I needed time to think of what to say. I got on the Stairmaster knowing I wouldn't run into him. I just watched him do his weights from my high perch. My legs and arms moved slowly, filled with lead and dread.

After a while, I watched him pick up his bag and get ready to leave. "Happy New Year's,"

I whispered, knowing I wouldn't see him until Wednesday, the longest I had been without seeing him in a while. I didn't see him go out. Where did he go?

I heard my name and looked down. There he was, looking up at me with those adorable grey eyes. I melted.

He came to talk to me? He's never not gone directly out once he picked up his bag.

I looked down into his eyes.

"Are you going to go to Vermont?" he asked.

"Yes," I sighed. "I feel like I have to for the kids. Haley wants a vacation and I hate to be selfish and say no."

"Go, you'll have fun. When will you be back?" he asked.

"Tuesday, I think. Why?"

He just stared at me. "No reason," he finally said. He shifted his bag to his other shoulder. "Have a good time."

"I will," I said. I watched his hot little butt leave.

Don't go! I wanted to scream. Take me with you. Don't make me go to Vermont. I would rather stay here with you. PLEEEEEEEEEEAAAAAAAASE!!!!

I watched until he turned the corner out of view.

Oh well. That wasn't supposed to end that way.

I put my sad song *letting go* on my iPhone and sang to myself. I wondered how I would get through the next four days without seeing Larry.

10 Vermont—What Am I Going To Do?

Jack, Jesse, Haley and I left for Vermont later that day. I brought my computer to finish my book before New Year's. We arrived in the late afternoon. There was three feet of snow on the ground. Our hosts, Sam and Betty, were not there yet. There was a note on the door saying to go in. We dragged in all our stuff.

The house was old and musty, and we could hear the squirrels and mice in the walls. Haley looked at me. "Why did I want to come here?" she asked.

"Because you thought it would be fun and you didn't want to stay home."

"Oh, well I didn't know it would be like this," she said.

"Well, we'll just have to make the best of it," I answered.

Jesse, Jack and Haley went skiing, but since I don't love it and didn't have the clothes for it, I chose not to spend seventy-five dollars a day on me. Sam and Betty had arrived, so Betty and I went for a walk up the mountain. The second day I knew the way, so I went by myself.

I crunched up the mountain, my mind spinning. I had no happy ending. Why did I ever think Larry was interested? I rehashed every conversation we had, wondering if each nuance meant something. I had only seen him once outside the gym when we met for coffee at Dunkin' Donuts. All he did was ask about Jack. He called me once, and it was about getting his friend a job.

Why did I think there was any interest on his part? He was nice and validated my feelings, but that didn't mean he had any romantic interest in me, did it?

I slid in the snow, catching myself so I didn't end up on my butt. I was doing the same thing I had done with Tom, creating a fantasy in my mind that had no basis in reality. Somehow, it seemed I needed to. My real life was so unpleasant that it was the only thing that made me feel better. I didn't want to numb myself with food and alcohol, and the fantasy seemed like it was less damaging. Anyway, who did it really hurt?

I checked the time. I wasn't ready to go back and be stuck in that little, musty house, so I kept going.

Why do I need to create these fantasies?

I was getting tired walking uphill in the deep snow. A bunch of snow fell from the trees onto my head, reminding me of a Disney princess cartoon.

"I want a fairy tale," I said out loud. "Of course."

If I found true love, all my problems would be solved, and my life would be perfect. Oh my God. That's what I used to think would happen when I lost weight. All my problems would be solved. I've been thinking Larry was the one who would save me. Why? I wondered.

A memory nagged at my head. As I walked, breathing hard, it came to me. The fantasy relationship with Paul McCartney made me feel safe, secure and loved unconditionally.

I guess I'm still having them, I thought.

I felt the tears building inside my cheeks. I had created a fantasy life with Paul, then Tom, and now with Larry. In my mind, I was accepted and valued, not criticized. It was safe and there was no stress.

I continued up the mountain, enjoying the snow-covered woods all around me. I watched the breath come out of my mouth. Even though these relationships lived completely in my mind, they made me happy. It felt like the only place I could really be myself.

I guess I had decided when I was four years old that no one could really love me. The only place I could be loved was in my mind, in my fantasies. I could have anything I wanted there. And the prince would finally save me. He would love me as I was, and I would finally have my dream.

But did this prevent me from living in my own real life?

Or was it protecting me from the feelings I was trying to suppress or numb?

I was no longer a little girl. I didn't live in a castle and there weren't eight dwarfs or a prince who was coming. Where did that leave me?

I kept walking and thinking.

It was easier to live there than to think about how I didn't have an answer for my relationship with Jack. I knew I wasn't happy with him, but the thought of divorce terrified me. I just couldn't go there yet.

I stepped on a branch and started to fall. Somehow, I caught myself and didn't go down.

Phew, that was close.

I checked my watch—45 minutes.

Uh oh. I better start back.

I turned around to walk down the mountain. It was harder on my knees since the mountain was steep here. How was I going to make it down?

One step at a time, I told myself.

Had I gotten anywhere? If I put men and fantasies aside, for the moment. I continued to climb down the mountain, noticing I was no longer cold.

I pictured a short-haired, overweight woman with baggy jeans and an oversized t-shirt coming down the escalator at the mall three years before and my eyes filled with tears.

That poor girl, I thought. *So stuck and so unaware.*

I struggled to breathe. I couldn't believe I thought my only problem was weight. I wiped the tears away with my hand.

How did I let myself get that way? Why? What had happened to me?

I searched in my pockets for a tissue. All I had was a scrap.

This was not going to be good.

No sense dwelling on the past. I needed to focus on the progress I'd made.

I had lost 32 pounds. I was an athlete again and took care of myself. I dressed better and had grown out my hair. I had completed a triathlon. I felt like a contender again, instead of a fat, invisible mom on the playground. I had taken control of my finances. I had my own bank account and had started saving money. I no longer felt powerless and victim to Jack's spending habits. I had friends again, was doing things, being successful at work, and enjoying my life. And, I was finishing a book. A lifelong dream was being fulfilled.

I turned onto the street where Sam and Betty's house was. The road was not plowed, and it was harder to step.

Almost there.

Even though there was work to do relationship-wise, I was in pretty good shape. I was on my way. I was not where I wanted to be, but I was not where I was.

I shook the snow off my boots and walked into the ski house.

FINDING THE OLD HILARY AGAIN

11 You're Kidding!

The first day back at the gym after the New Year's holiday, I saw Larry stretching. I was about to walk away without saying anything, just to pay him back for not being interested, but I changed my mind. Why shouldn't we be friends?

I got a mat and put it down next to him.

"Hi," I said.

"Oh, hi," he said looking up. "How was your weekend?"

"I survived. It was long. But I'm excited because I finished my book."

"Good for you," he said, turning over to lie on his back.

You're still adorable, I thought. Why am I so happy when I am next to you? Why does my heart keep beating so fast? Oh, stop it. He is SO not into you. Just leave it as stretching friends at the gym. That's it.

I was exhausted from all the hours of torturing myself over him all weekend.

"Hey," he said. I turned to look at him. He was looking right at me with those adorable grey eyes.

"What?" I asked.

He looked me right in the eyes for a minute. Looking away, he said, "The reason I asked you if you were going to Vermont was because I had some time and wanted to get together with you for a couple of hours that day."

You've got to be kidding, I thought.

"Shit. Why didn't you tell me that? I would have stayed home."

"I didn't want you to. You had to go for the kids. I understand that."

"Well, I would have wanted to stay." I pulled my leg closer to my chest.

Damn. So much energy wasted.

"It's ok. I understand. We'll have another chance."

Are you sure? It's taken him a year to get this far. Why didn't I know this? I could have had a good weekend instead of spending four days trying to get over him. The good news is he wants to spend time with me outside the gym. Maybe it's not a fantasy. Maybe he does like me....

12 One Month Later

I turn the handle. The door opens. Slowly, I peer in.

"Oh my God," I screech. "It's still here. It's the massage room."

The massage room at the gym looks like it has been frozen in time. It looks like the last masseuse just walked out and didn't take anything with her. The bed is fully made. The oils are there. The towels are laid out.

"Wow," I say to Larry. "My sexual fantasy takes place in this room. I have been picturing wild things in this room for three years. I can't believe it's still here and exactly the same way it is in my mind."

"Well, let's not waste any time," he says, starting to pull down his pants.

I just stare. I can't believe what I am seeing. I haven't seen an erection like that since… well, for a long time. I can't move. I froze.

Think! my brain was screaming. *What do I do?*

"Do you have a condom?" I blurted.

"No," he said, pulling up his pants. He hesitated for a split second.

"Forget it."

He started pushing me out the door. I leaned back against him. I could feel the bulge I had just witnessed, pressing against my butt. Erotic and memorable.

I couldn't believe I had blown it.

THINK! *my brain was screaming at me.*

I have dreamt of this moment. Don't waste it totally.

"Wait," I said breathily, "Can I at least have a kiss?"

"But I'm all sweaty," he said.

"I don't care," I whispered. I pushed him back into the room.

I leaned forward and our lips met. His lips were soft and nice. The kiss was sweet, and full of promise. I sighed as he backed away.

Wow! I thought.

"Come on," he said, pushing me out. "Let's go stretch."

"Ok," I said, dreamy eyed….

EPILOGUE

Four years later, I am sitting in my beach cottage staring at the Long Island Sound. I can't believe I have a place of my own on the water. So much has happened. Jack and I finally got divorced a year and a half ago.

It was difficult standing up to his arguments about why divorce was a bad idea, but I stayed strong until the papers were signed. Since then, we have talked through much of what happened. He did a lot of work on himself and apologized for the way he treated me.

I let much of my hostility go and saw my part in the demise of our marriage. We have become friends again. We are partners in raising our kids. He is very supportive in my transformation, and I no longer resent him.

I walk down the stairs to my private beach. It's only several blocks from where Larry and I spent a lot of time for a couple of summers. After I got separated, I entered a passionate, emotion-filled relationship with him. I was the happiest I had ever felt in my life.

Then his wife found out about me. Yes. He had a wife. He had lied to me for years about being divorced. That was the end of that. And that was tough.

I had a hard time accepting that my loving, validating, fun best friend was not the person he had pretended to be. I didn't want to admit how wrong I was about him. And how fooled I had been. And I didn't know why it was so hard.

I finally admitted that once again I was holding onto a fantasy. I had gone from numbing myself with food and alcohol, to numbing myself with the empty promises of a dishonest man. As long as I fooled myself, I could still think he was going to save me. I didn't have to be responsible for myself and my life. I didn't have to be uncomfortable.

I was also disturbed that once again; I had fallen for a man who lied and wasn't available. It was a pattern that I thought I had broken when I got married. Obviously, I hadn't.

It taught me that I CAN trust my instincts the next time something doesn't seem right. And I can speak up and have what I want. I don't have to put up with bad behaviors or constant disappointments. It was a hard lesson to learn, but I am grateful that now I will be more aware.

I walk into the water and watch the sand fall around my feet. Letting go of my attachment to Larry was one of the hardest things I had ever had to do. But I knew I needed to move on in order to start dealing with my real life.

I mended my relationship with my son, Jesse, and became his mother again. It wasn't easy to hear him tell me that he felt like I had deserted him when he was little. I had. I thought he was Jack's. I apologized and he forgave me. We have since gotten very close. He is an amazing boy who is thriving in college.

Haley and I have had our ups and downs like most mothers and daughters, but we still have that special bond. She is also flourishing in college. When she calls me her best friend I feel like the luckiest mother in the world.

I walk a little further and look out over the other beach houses near me. I feel a pang of longing for the fantasy days with Larry.

Stop it, this is your real life. What else can you be proud of?

I stopped blaming my parents and Jack for my unhappiness. They all did the best they could. No one was consciously trying to hurt me. It's on me now. Forgive and move on.

Sometimes I still want that outside validation. I can feel myself going into a panic. I stop, breathe, try to relax and realize that I am fine. I don't need anyone else to tell me I am okay. I can do that myself. I can trust myself and have faith that I am on the right path.

I start walking past my cottage and toward the other end of the beach. A seagull flies right in front of me. I know I still have plenty of work to do. But I know one thing: I am not that girl on the escalator, overweight, asleep, and just getting through each day. I wasn't even aware that I had given up on myself.

I have to remember my progress. It seems now that it was easy to do what I did, but I

EPILOGUE

need to remember the struggle, so I don't take any of it for granted.

I started Weight Watchers in 2010. I was not one of the fast losers. It took me two years to lose my 34 pounds to get to lifetime. I was not a superstar there. My body is now 30 pounds lighter, and I'm fit. I have maintained most of my weight loss for four years. I have never missed a week of getting weighed. I don't know anyone else who can say that.

I know how to work out. I am disciplined. I am healthy and strong. I feel good about how I look. I have a talented hair person who does my color and cut. I dress comfortably when I want, and I have a work wardrobe that I feel professional and attractive wearing. That is a miracle.

I turn around to admire my new neighborhood.

I think of my visit to the financial planner a few weeks before. We had been crunching numbers for hours and I was frustrated and tired.

All of a sudden, he looked up and said, "You did it."

"Did what?"

"You did what you wanted to do."

"What?" I asked impatiently, eager to get out of there.

He stared at me again, his smile getting bigger.

"You took Haley on the vacation you had promised her, to Hawaii no less. You have savings, you are putting money away for retirement, and you have a positive cash flow. That's what you told me you wanted. You did it."

I just stared at him while it sunk in. Then, of course, I burst into tears. Several years before my life had consisted of watching for negative balances to try to minimize our overdraft fees.

I had turned things around. Another miracle.

My phone buzzed. It was one of my friends. We had been close since our 50th birthday party reunion. I have quite a few friends that I can call or go out with now. What a difference from my own 50th birthday party when I couldn't find more than three friends to invite.

Another dream had been to create communities of people where I was loved, supported and accepted. I did that too.

Climbing up my stairs and seeing my bills on the table, I was calm. I have money in my account to pay them. What a difference from a few years before. I just finished the best quarter I ever had at AFLAC. I was about to receive the biggest bonus of my life.

My income increased every year due to my renewal income. I had never thought I would be self-sufficient again. Now I was, and it felt liberating.

I walk through my cottage appreciating the two decks, washer dryer and grill for cooking. I rent it for the exact price I was looking for. I had looked at more than 35 places. I could not see myself coming home to any of them. This cottage was a place that nourished my spirit and filled my soul.

I know in my heart that if I could create my home, I could create the rest of my life.

I look out at the water beyond my deck. The best gift is finally knowing that I am loved. No matter what. Flaws and all. Despite what others say and do.

That is my happy ending. A healthy, strong, loving relationship with myself.

Best of all, I have the freedom to have the second piece of French toast if I want it.

Made in the USA
Middletown, DE
09 December 2019